For all of us who know a
that her book, Splendid
Genesis to Revelation. I ... ... many Bible studies
included throughout each chapter, motivating us to study and
research further. All will desire to make this available to friends
and loved ones as we prepare for our Lord Jesus Christ's soon
return for His Bride. As the principles communicated in these
pages are truly lived out by every one of us who read them, this
book will be another catalyst for the end time revival we are all
expecting before that Splendid Day.

— *CAMILLA LEATHERS SEABOLT*
Former Executive Director of
Community Bible Study (1997-2013)

Splendid Day by Mary Soler is not only TIMELY reading—it
is ESSENTIAL reading! For those who still believe time is
standing still by the sheer willpower of their unyielded hearts,
this book might not be for you. For those who know otherwise,
and are willing to "roll up the sleeves" of their spiritual house
and garments, you will feel compelled to share its enriching
contents with every one you know and love. Sharing it with all
who search for a genuine transformational change that is not
mere hype. This page turner is divinely instructed, persuasive
and convincingly urgent, drawing to the deeper things of God.
Grab it, read it, re-read it, use it, and reference it for as long as
we are given one second more in this life, and unquestionably
before the sure arrival of Him who offers you entry into the
eternal life to come!

— *HEATHER TAYLOE*
Co-Founder, Strategic Communications Group
Voice of Hope World Radio Network

Rather than a theological study, Mary Soler has chosen to present "The greatest love story ever told" in a fresh, concise way. Both new believers and seasoned ministers alike can't help but be drawn into a stronger and deeper relationship with Christ. This timely book is destined to impact readers around the world.

– STEVE AND VARVAH ALLEN
Co-Founders of Hearts of Fire International

As a Jewish woman, I appreciate Mary Soler's in-depth understanding and usage of the metaphors contained in the Word of God in their Hebrew context. She makes it clear, as with a job description, that we need to have a good understanding about our role and responsibilities as the Bride. This particular "marriage" should be guarded, watered, and nurtured faithfully and diligently.

As a believer, I'm so glad Mary chose not to avoid or water-down the harder aspects of God's Word for our lives. She sees the vital importance these "rules" play in our lives, forming us to be the human beings God intended us to be and bringing about true peace and joy that can only come from the truth.

As a woman, I am grateful for her transparency as she allows the Lord to use her own story to illustrate ours. Mary masterfully weaves the truth of the Bible with her own poignant, personal failure, redemption and lessons learned, giving her the authority to speak these timeless truths into our lives. Her approach to explain His love for us makes me love how I am loved.

– CORRY KEELER
Director, Lev Shelo Ministries
Journalist for the Messianic Times

This thought-provoking book encompasses the entire Bible with divine foreshadowing of our eternal marriage to Christ. Comparing Old Testament Jewish wedding traditions to our future wedding to our Bridegroom Jesus Christ, Mary Soler describes the divine process of salvation, sanctification, and righteousness to prepare us for the Rapture. To help readers connect on a deep and heartfelt level, Mary shares honestly and with profound vulnerability about her own struggles and victories, touching the hearts of all who have sinned and fallen short of the glory of God.

– *SHANNAE ANDERSON, PH.D.,*
Adjunct Professor at Fuller Theological Seminary
Christian Clinical and Forensic Psychologist

Splendid day is a marvelous reminder of the greatest event the world will one day experience—the return of Christ. Mary Soler's book is full of fresh revelation and encouragement for all believers to step into the preparation necessary to be ready for Christ's return, and to do the work God has called us to do until He does!

– *SAMUEL GALLUCCI*
Senior Pastor, Embrace! Church
CEO, The Kingdom Center

ISBN 978-1-7376909-0-0 (paperback)

ISBN 978-1-7376909-1-7 (e-book)

Published in association with Jessica Suggs Marketing, Chandler, AZ 85248.

Cover design: E+M Creative Studio

Author photo: Debbie Walton Photography

Interior design: Jessica Suggs Marketing

Printed in the United States of America

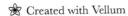 Created with Vellum

SPLENDID DAY

HOW TO LIVE EXPECTANT AND READY TO MEET JESUS

MARY SOLER

with
JOSEPH SOLER

DEDICATION

This book is dedicated to my Eternal Husband, Jesus, and my earthly husband, Joseph. Both of whom continue to show me unconditional, covenantal love. I would not be the person I am today without the two of you. I am forever grateful.

ACKNOWLEDGMENTS

To my amazing family—my husband, Joseph, and adult children Sophia, Alyssa, Marcus, and their spouses. Your continual
love and support over the years have meant the world to me. I
am beyond blessed to be a wife, mother, and grandmother, and·
thankful that God thoughtfully placed each one of you in my
life. You and your children are the joy of my life! My heart is
full.

To my Community Bible Study and Calvary Community
Church family—Thank you for the great privilege to teach
God's Word in and through you for so many years. Your sacred
trust in me has been immeasurable.

To our special friends who believed in me enough to bring the
radio program "Return of the King" to fruition—you know
who you are.

To Laura and Tom—who God used to encourage me to write
my first book.

To Carolyn Landers, who came alongside me to give me a push-start; my sister Angela Gober who continually cheered me on from the sidelines; and Jessica Suggs who ran the last lap with me to bring this book across the finish line.

To all of you who co-labored alongside me as I taught God's Word over the years in CBS and my local church. Your love, friendship, and hunger to pursue Jesus and serve Him well was a blessing and always inspired me.

Lastly, for the immense honor to be a vessel the Lord would use. I am humbled. "Not to us, LORD, not to us but to Your name be the glory, because of Your love and faithfulness." — Psalm 115:1

CONTENTS

splendid; adjective [1]

1: possessing or displaying splendor: such as
    a: shining, brilliant
    b: marked by showy magnificence
    2: illustrious, grand
    3: excellent
    a: being out of the ordinary

INTRODUCTION

So you also must be ready, because the Son of Man will come at an hour when you do not expect Him.
— Matthew 24:44

ARE YOU EXPECTANT?

It's been over 2,000 years since Christ walked on this earth. As Savior, Lord, and heavenly Bridegroom, Jesus left with a promise to return for His Bride, the Church. Since then, generations have expectantly watched and waited for that *Splendid Day* to arrive. Today more than ever, prophetical events indicate that the Rapture is soon to occur. Although no one can know the exact day or hour when Jesus will return for His Church, believers can and should make themselves ready. Sadly, Jesus indicates only half will be prepared.

In a frank discussion with His disciples about His promised return, Jesus tells the Parable of the Ten Virgins. All ten knew with certainty that the bridegroom was coming. As was typical in Hebrew tradition, the bridegroom was expected to arrive in the dark of night. Five of the virgins wisely took time to secure the needed oil to light their lamps, while the other five foolishly did not.

Recognizing the time for the bridegroom's arrival was upon them, the entire bridal party took their lamps and ventured outside to wait. However, when the bridegroom appears, only five are ready. Their individual preparedness brought about a stark contrast of outcomes. One group is allowed to enter the grand festivities, while the other is locked out. The five virgins who were unprepared anxiously knocked at the door but were never admitted. Their slack in readiness cost them dearly.

Then in the first three chapters of Revelation, Jesus addresses the seven lampstand churches regarding the Last Days. Of the seven churches, five He rebukes, and only two does He fully commend. In these passages of Scripture, Jesus clearly prophesies that before He returns, an astonishing 71 percent of His Church will be living in compromise and apathy.

Did you catch that? Please don't miss it. It's time to stop and reflect. Which group do you align with? Hopefully, you are already expectant and well prepared to meet Jesus when He returns. However, many are not. There are also some who are prepared but carry deep concern for loved ones who have not yet accepted Christ as their Lord and Savior. Such concern is well founded. It is time for us, the Church, to wake up, clothe ourselves in the holiness Christ provides, fill our spiritual oil lamps, and lead others to do the same.

ARE YOU READY?

In our daily lives, we spend a lot of time getting ready. Most of us do quite a bit just to get ready for an ordinary day. We make an extra effort to get ready for a trip, a job interview, or an exam. If you think about it, much of life is spent in preparation. But undoubtedly, the one occasion in life that involves the most preparation and expense is a wedding. This is especially true for the Royal Wedding of the heavenly Bridegroom to His Church. But is this glorious event first and foremost in our hearts and are we preparing now, while we can?

This book is written to explain, encourage, and empower you to be ready for the coming of the Lord's Rapture and the wedding celebration that will follow. No dates are provided, of course. However, you will receive biblical teaching to help you understand the Church's role as Christ's Bride and your part in it. You will also receive practical steps that you and your loved ones can take to ensure that you'll be *confidently ready* to meet Jesus when He returns.

A perfect match for Father God's Son has been arranged in Heaven. The picture of a husband and wife is used throughout Scripture to describe this mysteriously beautiful union—a union where God's choice and man's free will intersect. To this end, Jesus began His public ministry at a wedding and concluded the Bible in the book of Revelation by spotlighting His stunningly radiant bride, the wife of the Lamb. It's no wonder that the whole of Scripture culminates with a beckoning from the Spirit and the Bride for the Bridegroom to "'Come!' And let the one who hears say, 'Come!'" (Revelation 22:17).

Do you hear it? *Are YOU ready* to join the impassioned call?

PART 1: WHAT IS THE SPLENDID DAY?

A MATCH MADE IN HEAVEN

The Bible is a wildly dynamic love story. At the very heart of it, the Heavenly Father has selected a Bride for His Son Jesus. This match made in Heaven is comprised of all the members of Jesus' worldwide Church over the ages, and He intensely desires to have Her forever at His side. There we will share His royal throne and be showered with eternal blessings.

This ideal was first presented in the book of Genesis, where God formed a wife for Adam saying, "It is not good for the man to be alone. I will make a helper suitable for him... Then the Lord God made a woman (Eve)... and He brought her to the man" (Genesis 2:18, 22).[1] It was here that the institution of marriage was established on earth. It provides a vivid picture of an even greater heavenly union that would one day come when Jesus returns to earth to gather his Bride.

With this understanding of the importance of the marriage bond, it should be unsurprising that Jesus began his public ministry at a *wedding* in Cana. Here, His premier miracle was changing *ordinary water* into *extraordinary wine*.[2] In doing so, the Son of God not only revealed His glory, but He also provided the key prophetic element of wine, which is used throughout the Hebrew betrothal, ceremonial wedding, and surrounding celebratory events.

These actions speak volumes about why Jesus came—to give the bride and guests what no other earthly bridegroom could give. He offered a new kind of wine, *a heavenly wine*. This new wine is seen flowing throughout Jesus' life, death, and resurrection, manifesting a full demonstration of His love for all those selected and fashioned by the Father to be Jesus' suitable helper—His Bride.

Described many times in Scripture as an unfaithful, promiscuous woman, Jesus' Bride is an unlikely choice, but she does not remain this way. With completed sacrificial love, Jesus wins her over and begins her transformation to make her pure and radiant, changing her just like He did the water—from ordinary into extraordinary. This love story, as penned throughout the pages of the Bible, culminates with the Bride yearning for her Beloved to whisk her away so she can be with Him forever. Restless for His return, in the last days she is heard exhorting in unity with the Holy Spirit for her Eternal Husband to "Come!"[3]

The Bible presents many relatable illustrations of Christ and the Church. There is the Good Shepherd and the sheep, the Vine and the branches, the Corner-Capstone and living stones, the High Priest and priestly believers, the King of Kings and citizens of the heavenly kingdom, the Head and the body, and the Bridegroom and the Bride. It is only in this last picture of a marital union where a uniquely intimate relationship is portrayed.

Because God uses what is familiar in the physical realm to help His people understand greater spiritual truths, earthly marriages are designed, in their best form, to model Christ's eternal love relationship with His Bride, the Church.

This relationship is lasting, fulfilling, and provides unsurpassed joy and peace. Because of this, the devil will do everything he can to mock and destroy what God has beautifully ordained.

A MODERN-DAY LOVE STORY

My first name is *Mary*. My husband's first name is *Joseph*. In his birthplace of Cuba, his mother dedicated him to the Lord while he was still in her womb and gave him the middle name of *Jesus*. With our combined names of "Mary, Joseph and Jesus," it sounds like the beginning of a match made in Heaven, doesn't it?

Joseph and I can honestly say that we are blessed with an amazing marriage. However, it has not always been that way. It has taken many years to be able to say this with confidence. Joseph and I deeply love the Lord and one another and are wholeheartedly committed to both. We treasure our children, their spouses, and our grandchildren, praying that they too experience healthy, God-honoring marriages similar to what we have come to enjoy.

Joseph and I met in college. I was a first semester freshman, and he was a senior looking forward to graduating. It was a rainy day in late November when I entered the student union building. As I ventured down the hallway, I saw him sitting quietly reading a newspaper. All he did was look up at me with his big brown eyes and smile. That was it. I immediately knew, "There is the man that I am going to marry!" For me, it was love at first sight.

Selecting a seat on an adjacent sofa, my thoughts swirled as to how to engage in conversation. As I waited patiently through every glance exchanged, suddenly he rolled up his newspaper and tucked it away. Afraid he was leaving, I broke the silence and said, "If you're going outside, be prepared to get wet!"

Returning another heart-melting smile, Joseph looked into my eyes and said what would prove to be foreshadowing first words, "I'm not going anywhere."

Ever since I was a young girl, I always knew I would marry a *Joseph*—often writing our names enclosed with a heart. When he revealed that his name *was* Joseph, it confirmed to my soul what Song of Songs 3:4 expresses, "I found the one my heart loves. I held him and would not let him go till I brought him to my mother's house..." Arriving home later that afternoon, I could hardly wait to tell my parents. Chuckling, they told me to slow down as they listened. "We'll see," they cautioned, but I was confident in what I knew. Joseph was the one!

Love at first sight does not always happen when two people meet, but as evidenced in our love story, sometimes it does. Our first date was a few weeks later, and we discussed marriage on our second. That night he said the words that would lead to his proposal, "I can't live without you." As Dr. Howard Hendricks once said, "Marriage is not finding the person with whom you can live but finding that person with whom you cannot live without." This proved true for Joseph and me.

On Valentine's Day a few months later, Joseph came to my house and asked my father for my hand in marriage. I remember my parents opening a bottle of wine to celebrate with a toast. Joseph was 21 years old, but I was only 18. I thought, "I'm too young to drink!", but we all lifted our glasses and took a sip. Nearly one year after we met, we married on October 20, 1979. As it turned out, that date would later catch our attention for reasons beyond our wedding day.

A STARRY SIGN IN THE SKY

Over the years, various scientists, astronomers, and theologians have looked to the stars in an effort to calculate the true date of the Savior's birth. Contrary to popular belief, it is not December 25th, which the world commonly celebrates. As a result of this research, many other dates have been offered of which any internet search will reveal. One of the dates happens to be our favorite—*October 20, 6 B.C.*[4]

Joseph and I had no idea that the wedding date we had serendipitously selected quite possibly coincided with the birth of Jesus. Giving spiritual application to this thought has helped us view our marriage as more than an earthly match. Indeed, for us, it is a true match made in Heaven—a match that God ordained before either Joseph, or I were born. King David gave voice to this thought when he said, "All the days ordained for me were written in your book before one of them came to be" (Psalm 139:16b).

Does the fact that Joseph and I may have married on the same month and day of Jesus' birth make us any more special than you or anyone else? The answer is "No." However, because God can use what is in the physical realm to help His people understand greater spiritual truths, it is our sincere desire that He will consecrate the story of our marriage and use it to point others to the ultimate match made in Heaven. A match that far supersedes and transcends our own—that of Christ to His Bride, the Church. Through the coming pages, we hope that you too will clearly see that the story of *your life* has also been consecrated and established in the heavens above.[5]

THE MULTIPLICATION OF GOD'S LOVE

At some timeless moment, God decided that He did not want to live without you or me, so He prearranged an eternal union. The love He has for each person He created is beyond our comprehension. It is a love that is everlasting and motivated by kindness.[6] As a triune God, He is One—existing as three distinct Persons: God the Father, God the Son and God the Holy Spirit. Each Person of the Godhead is the same in nature and perfect in relationship to the other.[7]

First John 4:8 tells us that "God is love," and just as a married couple often wishes to multiply their love by adding to their family with children, so too, God's love is not limited to the Trinity. God *chose* to create the heavens and the earth, as well as man in His image—to love and to be freely loved. Together, God and man were destined to enjoy everything He created, and when the act of creation was completed, God said, "it was very good."[8] It's important to take notice that *God's choosing came before His making.* Love is always a choice.

The Bible provides even greater insight revealing that God "chose us in Him before the creation of the world… In love He predestined us for adoption to sonship through Jesus Christ, in accordance with His pleasure and will" (Ephesians 1:4-5). Did you get that? Even before the creation of the world, before you or I were born or did anything good or bad, God loved us. His unwarranted, unearned, unconditional love is vastly different from romantic love, and far exceeds the experience of what we call "love at first sight." Instead, God's love can be better described as *"love at first thought."*

Romance is marvelous and can awaken one's soul, especially when it comes to that first kiss. Yet, if the truth be known, our first kiss isn't the one received on our lips by a boyfriend or girlfriend on the front porch. It isn't even the gentle kiss on the cheek by our mother or father on the day of our birth or adoption. Rather, our true first kiss happened the moment God the Holy Spirit took His *first thought* of us and then one day—tenderly breathed into our nostrils the awakening breath of life.[9] This is a pure kind of love for which King David poeticized, "For You created my inmost being; You knit me together in my mother's womb. I praise You because I am fearfully and wonderfully made" (Psalm 139:13-14).

Each person has been lovingly formed by God with the intention that we come to know Him personally. Reciprocating the love God extends is expressed only as we embrace the heavenly match the Father has set before us in His Son, Jesus. In our free will, as we accept and receive Jesus Christ as Savior and Lord, we are then able to experience God's love fully and deeply. When God's choice and man's will intersect to establish the relationship, an incredible love story begins.

THE HEAVENLY BRIDEGROOM AND HIS BRIDE

The heavenly *Bridegroom* and *Bride* are first introduced in the New Testament by John the Baptist when he declared, "I am not the Messiah but am sent ahead of Him. The *bride* belongs to the Bridegroom. The friend who attends the *bridegroom* waits and listens for Him, and is full of joy when he hears the bridegroom's voice. That joy is mine, and is now complete" (John 3:28-29).

Similarly, Jesus confirms He is the Bridegroom by saying, "How can the guests of the Bridegroom mourn while He is with them? The time will come when the Bridegroom will be taken from them; then they will fast" (Matthew 9:15).

Later, in Ephesians 5:23-27 and 32, the Apostle Paul clarifies who the mysterious Bride is by explaining:

For the husband is the head of the wife as Christ is the head of the Church, His body, of which He is the Savior... Husbands, love your

9

> *wives, just as Christ loved the Church and gave Himself up for her to make her holy, cleansing her by the washing with water through the Word, and to present her to Himself as a radiant Church, without stain or wrinkle or any other blemish, but holy and blameless... This is a profound mystery—but I am talking about Christ and the Church.*

Every member of Christ's diverse worldwide Church makes up His Bride. However, it is important to understand how God's Word further describes her. In this way, we can introspectively evaluate the virtues we should seek to embody in our own lives.

1. The Bride loves Jesus and keeps His commands. (John 14:21)
2. The Bride allows her Bridegroom to wash her clean with the Word. (Ephesians 5:25-26)
3. The Bride will be a radiant Church—holy without stain or wrinkle. (Ephesians 5:27)
4. The Bride readies herself for her Wedding Day. (Revelation 19:7)
5. The Bride is dressed and adorned with sacred bridal garments. (Isaiah 61:10)[10]
6. The Bride is as a pure virgin with sincere devotion to Christ. (2 Corinthians 11:2b, 3b)
7. The Bride is filled with the oil of the Holy Spirit. (Matthew 25:1-4)
8. The Bride is an intrinsic part of the Holy City, the New Jerusalem. (Revelation 21:2)

A WORD TO MEN AS CHRIST'S "BRIDE"

Being a member of the Bride-Church tends to be an easier concept for women who more naturally desire to be pursued, romanced, and wed. Being a bride is something a young girl may role play and perhaps see come to fruition when she exchanges wedding vows with her husband.

For men, it is a completely different story. As my husband, Joseph, dug deep into this topic, he confessed that he had a difficult time thinking of himself in this way. Below are his thoughts, and how he came to a place where he was able to embrace himself not only as a member of Christ's Church, but also the Bride.

JOSEPH SOLER WRITES:

For me as a man, being referred to in any way as a *bride* is a strangely foreign concept. After all, God generally wired men to be the initiators, leaders, providers, protectors, and pursuers in a love relationship.

Being a married man, I have experienced the joy of being the groom, standing beside *my bride* at the altar and exchanging vows before God and man. Then as the father of two daughters, I observed that from the time they were little girls, they dreamt of one day meeting the man of their dreams and getting married. In time, I had the great pleasure as *father of the bride* of walking them both down the aisle and giving them away in marriage.

One thing I have come to appreciate though is that despite our different gender roles, Scripture teaches that we are all equal in the eyes of God, for "There is neither Jew nor Greek, neither slave nor free, nor is there male and female, for you are all one in Christ Jesus" (Galatians 3:28).

Our family bloodlines, race, social status, or gender is

inconsequential to God. What is of consequence is our relationship by faith in His Son Jesus Christ. As a result, "whoever is united with the Lord is one with Him in spirit" (1 Corinthians 6:17). This joining with the Lord Jesus is both spiritual and organically physical, NOT SEXUAL; however, it brings a level of intimacy that is unsurpassed![11]

The term *husband* is derived from an Old English word meaning "to dwell; to steward; to manage prudently." In Hebrew, the term husband means "man, servant, champion, great man." Interestingly, there is nothing sexual in either definition of the word husband. The meaning is all about dwelling together and caring valiantly for another. The role of *Eternal Husband* is something God jealously desires us to recognize and receive Him as, but we must first respond to His advances of love and His relentless pursuit of us.

Consider how every husband should know his wife intimately and better than anyone else. What she may think, how she may feel, and in what manner she is likely to react to things. With kind intentions, he is the one who is best able to love, comfort and counsel her in ways no one else can. And so, it is with the Lord, regardless of our gender.

King David was a man's man, rough and tumble. He was a warrior king, a deep and cherishing lover of women. He also had a binding love for his close friend Jonathan, but he loved God even more. Attracted to the beauty of the Lord, David wrote how he longed to dwell in perfect union and intimate fellowship with Him—even as a bride is with her husband.

HE EXPRESSED his feelings in Psalm 27:4-5b:
One thing I ask from the LORD,
this only do I seek:
that I may dwell in the house of the LORD
all the days of my life,
to gaze upon the beauty of the LORD
and to seek Him in His temple.
For in the day of trouble
He will keep me safe in His dwelling…

I ENCOURAGE you to take notice of David's use of the word LORD. In Hebrew, the word LORD is *Yehovah*[12] or *Jehovah*, which is the relational proper name of God. However, in Greek,[13] David's use of the word *LORD* is defined as "to whom a person belongs, about which he has the power of deciding."[14]

LORD is one of the names that men who love Jesus are comfortable calling Him. Even Sarah, addressed her earthly husband, Abraham, as "lord."[15] Both David and Sarah provide examples that both men and women can follow in recognition of Jesus' personal relationship with them, as well as His husbandly lordship over their lives.

ARRANGED MARRIAGES

The Church is comprised of both men and women and has been selected to be Jesus' Bride through an arranged marriage. In the last decade, matchmaking television programs have grown in popularity. One such reality show is called *Married at First Sight* where six people agree to legally marry a complete stranger that experts deem a perfect match. The first time the couple meets is at the altar.

seem like a novel idea in today's Western culture, marriages have been practiced since ancient , especially in the East. Because much of the Bible is written in the context of the Hebrew culture, it is important to understand the common practices and imagery that is portrayed regarding the matrimony of two Hebrew people, and how it parallels Christ's covenantal relationship with His Church.

The first stage of the Hebrew marriage process is called the *Shiddukhin* and refers to the preliminary actions that lead up to a legal betrothal. Sometimes, for the purpose of familial or political alliances, a matchmaker or *Shadkhan* would be used to select a bride, but more commonly the responsibility would belong to the *groom's father.* Although input could be given, it was ultimately the father's choice as to who would make a suitable wife for his son. Once a girl was identified, the young man would then go with his father to the potential bride's home to meet with *her father* in hope of securing the match.

In this same way, with the blessing of His Father, Jesus came down to earth, the home of the Bride-Church in order to secure His eternal match with us.

THE BETROTHAL

To gain the approval of the girl's father, a generous *bride-price* would be presented. This was often accumulated over a period of years to ensure that it would be more than sufficient. Once accepted, the girl's father would then proceed to carefully read through a prepared marriage contract called a *Ketubah.* The Ketubah outlined the rights and protections of the bride, as well as the groom's promised economic and social responsibilities to her as a husband. If the terms were agreeable, the man would then call for his daughter to seek her consent before proceeding. The final decision to accept or reject the proposal of marriage was hers alone.

The Bible outlines the many rights, protections, and blessings that are available to all who come under Christ's lordship. To either accept or reject Jesus' proposal of love to enter the eternal covenant, purchased with the bride-price of His blood, is the sole decision of every individual.

During the betrothal process, the groom would provide a skin of wine which would be poured out and offered to the bride as a *cup of acceptance* from which both would partake. These actions, along with the signing of the Ketubah in the presence of witnesses, would seal a man and woman's marriage covenant to one another.

The cup of acceptance used in the betrothal process foreshadowed the partaking of wine at the Last Supper. There, Jesus established the sacrament of Holy Communion with His Church as a remembrance of their eternal covenant to one another.[16]

In the Hebrew tradition, once a couple is betrothed, they are considered committed to one another as husband and wife. The betrothal period usually lasted one year and gave ample time to prepare their wedding garments and future home. During this time, the couple was prohibited from consummating the marriage. Their betrothal could only be broken by a certificate of divorce.[17]

The Bride-Church is currently in the betrothal stage—as consecrated for the heavenly Bridegroom. During this time, each member should be about the business of spiritually preparing themselves for the day of the Rapture when we will meet Jesus face to face. Meanwhile, Jesus is in Heaven preparing our eternal home. [18]

*

BRIDAL GIFTS

The cup of acceptance ceremony would be followed by the blowing of the shofar to officially announce the betrothal to the community. It was a joyful trumpet sound. Afterwards, the bridegroom would present costly gifts to his bride such as jewelry, oils, or spices as a good faith measure of his love and preparation for their wedding day.

The valued bridal gift Jesus gives to each member of His Bride-Church is the treasured Holy Spirit. Paul assures us with these words in Ephesians 1:13-14,

> *And you also were included in Christ when you heard the message of truth, the gospel of your salvation. When you believed, you were marked in Him with a seal, the promised Holy Spirit, who is a deposit guaranteeing our inheritance until the redemption of those who are God's possession.*

A NEW HOME IN THE FATHER'S HOUSE

After the ceremonial festivities, the bridegroom would depart the bride's home with a verbal promise that he would return one day to take her to their new home. Their new home was typically a room or chamber that he would *add on* to his father's existing house.

This same promise was verbally given by Jesus to His disciples the evening of the Last Supper after the wine cup of acceptance was ceremonially shared. John 14:1-3 recounts the scene. Shortly after partaking of the bread and wine at the Last Supper, Jesus assured His disciples saying,

> *"Do not let your hearts be troubled. You believe in God; believe also in Me. My Father's house has many rooms; if that were not so, would I*

have told you that I am going there to prepare a place for you? And if I
go and prepare a place for you, I will come back and take you to be with
Me that you also may be where I am."

The process of preparing the couple's new home would take approximately one year to complete. During which the father of the groom would provide guidance and supervision in its progress. He alone would determine when the house was completed and subsequently give permission for his son to go and fetch his bride so the wedding festivities could commence.

In the same way, only God the Father knows when He will send Jesus to return for His Bride. We see this evidenced in Mark 13:32, "about that day or hour no one knows, not even the angels in Heaven, nor the Son, but only the Father."

The tradition of married couples living alongside a groom's parents is rarely adopted in today's American culture; however, some embrace it out of desire or necessity. As the second child of four, I was the first to marry. In time, my siblings would follow, and a new generation of babies were born.

Our mother demonstrated her tireless love by faithfully serving her family in preparing beds, cooking, cleaning, and babysitting grandchildren when we would come and stay for visits. On the other hand, our father demonstrated his love by filling the house with music from his accordion and speaking treasured words of affirmation into each of our lives. Dad would also make repeated comments about how much he loved his children, their spouses and what would become their fourteen grandchildren. Dad wanted to be surrounded by all of us all the time and even spoke of *adding-on* to their existing house, so we could all permanently live together. This would often invoke a comical look from my mother as if to say "Yikes!"

What we can appreciate is that the uncompromising true love of our Bridegroom Jesus toward His Bride *originated* in the pure love of the Father's heart. It is truly His desire that one day *all* His children will live with Him and His Son *all* the time in their heavenly home forever. And one day we will!

CHAPTER 1 REFLECTION

1. You have been chosen by God the Father and pursued by the Son for the purpose of entering an eternal union with Him. Can you think of a time when you were aware of God's pursuit? What feelings are provoked?

2. Does it change the way you view yourself and your intrinsic value?

3. Read Psalm 139 and write down any words or phrases that are meaningful to you.

4. If you have not already accepted God's proposal of covenantal love, and you would like to do that now, a suggested prayer is provided in Appendix C at the back of this book.

FRACTURED FAIRY TALE

Now the serpent was more crafty than any of the wild animals the LORD God had made. He said to the woman, "Did God really say, 'You must not eat from any tree in the garden'?"

The woman said to the serpent, "We may eat fruit from the trees in the garden, but God did say, 'You must not eat fruit from the tree that is in the middle of the garden, and you must not touch it, or you will die.'"

"You will not certainly die," the serpent said to the woman. "For God knows that when you eat from it your eyes will be opened, and you will be like God, knowing good and evil."

When the woman saw that the fruit of the tree was good for food and pleasing to the eye, and also desirable for gaining wisdom, she took some and ate it. – Genesis 3:1-6

PARADISE LOST

God originally provided a wondrous paradise as home for Adam and Eve to dwell with Him. The Garden of Eden was earth in its perfection. The word *Eden* is derived from a Sumerian word meaning *plain* and is closely related to an Aramaic root meaning *fruitful, well-watered*. Both provide the image of an incredibly lush wonderland. In Hebrew, Eden[1] is also associated with the word pleasure. Using these combined meanings, the Garden of Eden has been interpreted to be a *paradise of pleasure.*[2] This land was filled with an abundance of resources for the first man and woman to enjoy, including robust trees with fruit for them to eat, a river running through the land watering the gardens, gold, aromatic resin, and onyx to name a few.[3]

If all that was not enough, God's first recorded words to man were *"You are free..."* And free they were for they were both naked, and they felt no shame.[4] Living in freedom with God, in a perfect habitat, was the blessing God planned for humanity from the beginning of time. The story reads like the ultimate *fairy tale*, doesn't it? But it is far from fiction. There was only one restriction God ordered for protection, commanding Adam to "...not eat from the tree of the knowledge of good and evil, for when you eat from it you will surely die" (Genesis 2:17).

As the story unfolds, the devil presents himself as a serpent in the garden and successfully tempts Eve to eat the forbidden fruit. In turn, Eve convinces Adam to also partake. Both ate the fruit from the tree of the knowledge of good and evil and would suffer the consequences. Immediately they were filled with shame for what they had done, and the "eyes of both of them were opened, and they realized they were naked; so they sewed fig leaves together and made coverings for themselves" (Genesis 3:7). This original sin fractured the real-life fairy tale and as a result, death entered the world. No longer allowed to be immortally nourished from the tree of life, both man and woman were banished forever from the Garden. At one time we had it all, but now *paradise was lost.*

Eve's action in being led astray by the serpent is a poignant warning to the Bride-Church that she, too, is susceptible to compromised devotion to God. In 2 Corinthians 11:2-3, the Apostle Paul gives this warning to the Church:

> *I promised you to one husband, to Christ, so that I might present you as a pure virgin to Him. But I am afraid that just as Eve was deceived by the serpent's cunning, your minds may somehow be led astray from your sincere and pure devotion to Christ.*

It is vital to recognize that the devil's primary mode of deceit is to cause us to distrust that God has His very best in mind for us. Contrast God's first words to man, "You are free," to Satan's first words, *"Did God really say...?"* If the devil can provoke us to doubt what God has spoken, he can more successfully seduce us with momentary pleasures. Often Satan leads us to believe we are being unfairly held back by our Creator. In falling for his lies, we end up exchanging our God-given freedom for bondage.

The Bible says "...it was not Adam who was deceived, but the woman was deceived and became a wrongdoer" (1 Timothy 2:14, NASB). If Adam was not fooled as his wife was, then what was his fall? Before Eve was created, God directly gave Adam the one commandment to not eat from the tree of knowledge of good and evil. Receiving this restriction first-hand, not secondhand as Eve had, Adam knew exactly what God had warned and therefore could not be victimized. None-theless, when presented with the life-altering decision, Adam willingly chose to disobey.

Somewhere in between Eve and Adam's failure, there was a window of opportunity where Adam could have refused to eat the fruit, driven out the crafty serpent from the Garden and proactively sought God to reconcile. The conversation could have sounded something like this:

Adam: "God, please help! Eve was enticed by the lying serpent and ate the fruit You commanded not to eat."

God: "Eve will then die."

Adam: "But, God, I love her and don't want her to die!"

God: "Adam, you know that the wages of sin is death."

To which Adam *could* have said, "Then take me!"

ADAM COULD HAVE GALLANTLY OFFERED to substitute his life for Eve's. However, being a natural man of the earth and not a spiritual man from Heaven as Jesus is, Adam's sacrifice would have only been a temporary fix—for the perishable can never inherit the imperishable.[5] Instead, Adam fell from grace alongside Eve, which meant there was now no suitable human sacrifice for either. Mercifully—instead of imposing immediate death upon both of them, God provided a temporary blood covering for their sins through the skin of the first animal sacrifice.

This sacrifice would have to suffice until a more perfect, sinless, and lasting atonement through Christ would later be provided. First Corinthians 15:45-50 explains that Adam was a type of Jesus who was to come. For the first man, Adam, was from the dust of the earth, while the second man, Jesus, is from Heaven. The Man from Heaven was needed to save all of humanity now, and it would require the high price of Jesus' life. *Whereas the earthly husband did not lay down his life for his bride, the heavenly Bridegroom did.*

AN EARTHLY BRIDE-PRICE

In Western culture the idea of a bride-price seems almost offensive, suggesting that brides can be purchased as a piece of property. Certainly, modern mail-order brides are often viewed negatively as commodities for sale. However, in ancient times the bride-price was not at all considered demeaning or offensive. To the contrary! Valuable items such as silver, gold, livestock, clothing, or land were given as part of the betrothal process tangibly expressing a man's intentions as a gift for a woman's hand in marriage. An example of this can be seen in the biblical betrothal of Isaac to Rebekah, in which Rebekah was presented with gold, jewelry, and articles of clothing.[6]

If the bride-price was found lacking, a suitor could be turned away. However, if the man was of modest means and did not have anything to give in exchange for the bride's hand, he could instead offer his services for a determined number of years. The Bible records that Jacob worked a total of fourteen years for his two wives, Leah and Rachel.[7]

AN UNBECOMING CHOICE

Through Adam and Eve's grievous fall, sin and death entered the world, and the entire human race was mortally affected. Romans 5:12 explains that "…as sin entered the world through one man, and death through sin, and in this way, death came to all people, because all sinned…" In effect, at one time Jesus' promised Bride was a spiritually dead one. This goes against every sensibility in selecting a spouse. However, it does happen. There are true stories of freed persons marrying death row inmates.

As God is a God of life, He would never enter a covenant with death—much less an eternal covenant of marriage with someone who is spiritually dead. However, this is what we once were. Ephesians 2:1-2 explains,

…you were dead in your offenses and sins, in which you previously walked according to the course of this world, according to the prince of the power of the air, of the spirit that is now working in the sons of disobedience. (NASB)

The truth is cutting and clear. Apart from sinless Jesus,

every person who ever lived has rebelled and entered an agreement with the devil and death—metaphorically exchanging God's *kiss of life* for Satan's *kiss of death*. Judas betrayed Jesus with such a kiss, and though undeserving, Jesus freely accepted it on our behalf.[8] The heavenly Bridegroom's selfless actions would bring our death row pardon.

A DIVINE ANNULMENT

What was God's remedy to our terrible predicament? A divine annulment! In Old Testament law, there is a provision that allows a husband or father to nullify a binding oath his wife or daughter has taken.[9] This allowance is seen played out when the southern kingdom of Judah made a covenant of death with their sworn enemy of Egypt. However, as both Israel's spiritual Husband and Father, God stepped in to cancel it. Isaiah 28:18 records, "Your covenant with death will be annulled; your agreement with the grave will not stand."

The word *annulled* in the Greek is defined as *to cover, purge, cancel, make atonement.*[10] To break the agreement Christ's future bride made with death and rescue men and women from Satan's grip, an atonement of blood was required. Leviticus 17:11 is clear in this: "For the life of a creature is in the blood, and I have given it to you to make atonement for yourselves on the altar; it is the blood that makes atonement for one's life."

THE HEAVENLY BRIDE-PRICE OF BLOOD

The Old Testament is full of blood sacrifices. In the Garden of Eden, God performed the first sacrifice for Adam and Eve after they sinned, covering their newly aware nakedness and shame with the skin of an animal. In time, it would be through the administration of the designated Jewish high priest who would sacrifice countless animals for the temporary forgiveness of his sins, as well as for the sins of the nation of Israel. All pointed forward to the needed blood atonement Jesus would satisfy. Hebrews gives us this truth, "...He has appeared once for all at the culmination of the ages to do away with sin by the sacrifice of Himself. Just as people are destined to die once, and after that to face judgment, so Christ was sacrificed once to take away the sins of many" (Hebrews 9:26b-28a).

Jesus came down from Heaven when He was conceived by the Holy Spirit within the womb of the virgin Mary. He humbled Himself and put on human flesh and although tempted in every way as we are, He lived a sinless life as the perfect, unblemished Lamb of God.[11] During three years of public ministry, Jesus demonstrated before eyewitnesses that He was the Son of God through recorded miracles, wonders, and signs exercising His power and authority over the elements, nature, diseases, demons, the devil, and death.

At the age of thirty-three, Jesus would be betrayed, unjustly tried, and beaten beyond recognition. With each Roman scourge, His precious blood was spilled to the earth. Crucified on a cross and pierced on His side, Jesus would be emptied of even more life blood in complete fulfillment of the law that it is only by blood that sin can be atoned. Hebrews 2:14-17 speaks of the magnitude of what Christ did for us:

Since the children have flesh and blood, He too shared in their humanity so that by His death He might break the power of him who holds the power of death — that is, the devil — and free those who all their lives were held in slavery by their fear of death... For this reason He had to be made like them, fully human in every way...

When Jesus miraculously provided *heavenly wine* at the wedding celebration in Cana, it was a foreshadowing of the blood sacrifice He would provide one day. This wine-blood connection was distinctly made at the Last Supper. It is recorded,

> *While they were eating, Jesus took bread, and when He had given thanks, He broke it and gave it to His disciples, saying, "Take and eat; this is My body." Then He took a cup, and when He had given thanks, He gave it to them, saying, "Drink from it, all of you. This is My blood of the covenant, which is poured out for many for the forgiveness of sins."* (Matthew 26:26-28)

The sacrament of Holy Communion mirrors the cup of acceptance wine ceremony of the betrothal process. Participation by members of Christ's Bride-Church serves as a continuing sign and reminder that Jesus paid the extravagant bride-price by offering His very life and purchasing "for God persons from every tribe and language and people and nation" (Revelation 5:9).

EQUALLY YOKED IN CHRIST

There is a biblical principle for both parties entering a marriage or partnership to be equally yoked spiritually. Two believers who are married share common spiritual ground with Jesus that provides "a cord of three strands that is not quickly broken" (Ecclesiastes 4:12).

Paul warns of mismatches saying, "Do not be yoked together with unbelievers. For what do righteousness and wickedness have in common? Or what fellowship can light have with darkness?... What does a believer have in common with an unbeliever?" (2 Corinthians 6:14-15).

While it is preferable for those who follow Christ to be equally yoked, it is not uncommon for men and women from differing faith backgrounds to marry. If you are a believer married to an unbeliever, please don't take this as a call for

27

divorce. The Bible directs you to remain married if your spouse is willing. Although you do not know if your spouse will be saved, a special spiritual covering is provided for such a relationship so that your children will be holy.[12]

ON NOVEMBER 17, 1981, almost two years after Joseph and I were married, my brother, Samuel Gallucci, invited us to hear the evangelist Bill McKee speak in Burbank, California. Both my husband and I were regular church attenders, but by God's grace and appointment, it would be this evening that the good news of the Gospel penetrated our hearts for the first time. McKee's sermon was titled "Get right or Get left!"

The evangelist explained that God loves us and longs to have us dwell with Him as man once did in the Garden, but our sin separates us from Him, bringing death and a no-escape eternity in the fires of hell. God is holy and just and cannot turn a blind eye to rebellion by letting crimes go unpunished. However, He provided an escape clause in John 3:16 that famously reads, "For God so loved the world that He gave His one and only Son, that whoever believes in Him shall not perish but have eternal life."

Because Jesus, the Son of God, lived a spotless life, the grave had no claim on Him. After being unjustly crucified, He was resurrected on the third day according to what was written in the Scriptures. Now glorified in Heaven, Jesus is seated at the right hand of the Father and is coming again to take to Himself all those who belong to Him.

Near the end of the service, McKee led an eyes-closed prayer for all who desired to confess their sin and receive Jesus as their Savior. Those who sincerely prayed would cross over from spiritual death to life. I closed my eyes and prayed.

At the end of the prayer, we were invited to open our eyes

and, in a public profession of faith, stand. As I jumped to my feet, I looked to my right, and there standing beside me was my husband, Joseph. We were astonished at what just took place! The Lover of our souls touched both of our hearts at the same remarkable moment, as we individually responded, "Yes."

Our life journey indeed began as equally yoked husband and wife—joined by mutual *unbelief.* But that night by the undeserved grace of God, we were miraculously yoked together in Christ as we sat side by side—forever changed by mutual *belief.*

This was the single most transformational day of our lives where, individually, our names were written in the Lamb's Book of Life, our hearts were sealed by the Holy Spirit, and together we became members of *the body of Christ*—His Bride-Church.[13]

ADAM'S RIB

After Adam was created, a suitable wife was fashioned for him. God the Great Physician accomplished this through divine sedation, performing the first surgery by cutting into Adam's side. Genesis 2:21-23 describes the procedure:

> *He took one of the man's ribs and then closed up the place with flesh. Then the LORD God made a woman from the rib He had taken out of the man, and He brought her to the man. The man said, "This is now bone of my bones and flesh of my flesh; she shall be called 'woman,' for she was taken out of man."*

In Hebrew, the word *rib* means *side; chamber (of a temple); rib (of a man); beam or plank (used in an architecture structure).*[14] With great precision, God purposefully removed one member from

MARY SOLER

Adam's *side*, a rib, within his *bodily temple* to form a bride for him. If we apply the colloquialism "the bones of a building," Eve's structural being was literally built from one of her husband's bones.

This amazing picture of using Adam's rib foreshadowed the formation of Christ's wife, the Bride-Church. One who would be of His body by the same Spirit, walking closely beside Him, and nestled near to His heart.[15] Ephesians 5:23 reveals, "For the husband is the head of the wife as Christ is the head of the Church, His body, of which He is the Savior."

The Bible records that after Jesus died on the cross, the soldiers came to break His legs. Upon finding Him dead, they pierced His side with a blade. Both Adam and Jesus received a *cut* on the side of their bodies. As the word *covenant* comes from the ancient practice of *cutting an agreement,* these cuts symbolized their covenant of marriage with their future brides.

The cuts on Adam and Jesus' sides were also necessary to prepare their future brides. The Bible tells us, "when they came to Jesus and found that He was already dead, they did not break His legs. Instead, one of the soldiers pierced Jesus' *side* with a spear, bringing a sudden flow of *blood and water*" (John 19:33-34).

The Greek word for *side* is defined as *rib*.[16] The elements that poured from Jesus's side where He was pierced provided astounding imagery of what the heavenly Bridegroom had just accomplished through His death. As both blood and water flowed out over Jesus' rib, it symbolized complete atonement and cleansing for His bride.

There is great spiritual significance to the presence of blood and water:

BLOOD: "How much more, then, will the *blood* of Christ, who through the eternal Spirit offered himself unblemished to God, cleanse our consciences from acts that lead to death" (Hebrews 9:14).

WATER: "...Christ loved the Church and gave Himself up for her to make her holy, cleansing her by the washing with *water* through the Word" (Ephesians 5:25-26).

There is no greater love than to lay one's life down for another. Through Jesus' elective, sacrificial death, He proved He esteemed His beloved bride over Himself. Even in name, He did not refer to Himself as the "Groom-bride" but the "Bride-groom." Although exalted above all, Jesus does not lord Himself *over* us, but died in humility *for* us—because we needed a Savior.

FORSAKEN FIRST LOVE

Immediately after receiving Jesus as my Savior, I began sharing my newfound faith with family, friends, co-workers, and anyone who would listen. It was much like when I first met my husband, Joseph. I was crazy in love. He was all I could think about, talk about, and I wanted to be with him always. Now falling in love with Jesus, He was all I could think about, talk about, and I wanted to be with Him always.

My early years as a believer was a time of impassioned enthusiasm but also great immaturity. As I think back, I realize now that although I was saved by Christ's blood, I had not yet been washed by the water of His Word. This was problematic. I had yet to fully understand that my commitment to Jesus meant leaving behind my old life of sin. I had yet to understand the responsibility of applying His teachings to my life. I had yet to understand that it was not enough to receive Jesus as my *Savior*, but that I also needed to make Him my *Lord*.

As a business major, I graduated college and landed a job with a Big 8 CPA firm. On the first rung of the corporate ladder, I was required to travel out of state on extended trips to train for my new position. Some of the interactions I observed among many of the other trainees were shocking and usually involved coarse joking, alcohol, and sex. Sometime later I was hired by a well-known computer company.

Once again, there were long trips away from home from one week to as many as six weeks in length. In hindsight, I realized I had allowed myself to be placed in unwise situations. Slowly prioritizing my career ahead of my marriage, I started making dangerously poor choices, allowing the world to influence me more than my Bible. In doing so, I put our marriage in jeopardy.

With each trip, the sin that I once found appalling became more and more enticing. Galatians 6:1 warns, "...if someone is caught in a sin… watch yourselves, or you also may be tempted." I failed in this. I did not watch myself, guard my heart, or protect our marriage, and I began to slowly misplace my affections. Emotionally detaching from my true love, I found myself compromising myself with other men. What started out as "harmless" flirtations led me down a road to commit adultery by the age of 23.

This marked the beginning of a long road of guilt and tremendous shame. To make matters worse, I decided that I would take this sin to my grave. I was determined not to tell my husband. I did not want to lose our marriage. Instead, I chose to live as if nothing happened, which is impossible to do.

During this time, my husband Joseph was also struggling with his own season of sin. He shares his testimony in chapter 5 of this book. Both of us can attest that no one is without sin. Big or little, we all need to take responsibility and address our own failings before the Lord in humble repentance. Thankfully, He stands eager to forgive us when we do—promising that "If we confess our sins, He is faithful and just and will forgive us our sins and purify us from all unrighteousness" (1 John 1:9).

TO THOSE LAMENTING THE AFTERMATH OF SIN

I want to pause here and speak to those of you who have been betrayed by your spouse. To say "I am sorry" sounds insufficient, even to my ears. I have experienced firsthand the pain and toll it takes on a spouse and family. Infidelity is a selfish sin that inflicts the deepest wounds. In many cases it proves itself fatal. It can be a destroyer, and most marriages cannot survive it. Know that God understands the severity of this sin and offers you biblical grounds for divorce as a way out.

However, that is not God's first choice as He hates divorce, and the broken relationships that transpire as a result.[17] Instead, and if possible, we are called to reconciliation. This is achievable if there is sincere repentance by the adulterer and you and your spouse remain committed to the relationship, as you seek counsel and healing.

I eventually did share my sin with my husband, but it took many years of prayer and effort to regain Joseph's trust, allowing our relationship to mend. This did not come easy, but by the grace of God our relationship is fully restored. As of this writing, we are celebrating nearly 42 years of marriage. We chose to live out the truth of 2 Corinthians 5:18 that "All this is from God, who reconciled us to Himself through Christ and gave us the ministry of reconciliation."

I hope our story offers hope to many.

I also want to speak to those of you who, like me, were the one who was unfaithful. If you have not yet whole-heartedly repented before God, it is time. Breaking a covenantal vow is a serious matter that needs to be confessed openly and honestly not only to God, but also to your spouse. Seek the Lord in the manner and timing in which you should do this. Choose to be obedient to God's leading. I can tell you from experience that when any sin or fear is brought into the light, it will lose its power.

Be prepared. There will be difficult consequences, and there is no guarantee how things will turn out. You may lose your marriage. I feared being left as a single mother of three young children. However, purpose in your heart that *it will be enough* that you are now choosing to live your life Jesus' way rather than your own. Once you begin doing that, it will change your life forever. God will transform you. 2 Corinthians 5:14-15 exhorts:

> *For Christ's love compels us... and He died for all, that those who live should no longer live for themselves but for Him who died for them and was raised again.*

HOSEA'S WIFE

The Old Testament book of Hosea provides a fitting example of God's redemptive power over broken relationships. The prophet Hosea was commanded by God to do something unimaginable. He was to take a wayward, unfaithful wife for himself. Her name was Gomer. Gomer was a human metaphor for adulterous Israel whose sin was idolatry. God had made a covenant with the nation of Israel and was faithful in His love and commitment to her. But the response of his spiritual bride was instead to chase after the false gods of other nations.

Hosea's name means *salvation*. Hosea had every right to divorce Gomer, but in keeping with his name and the picture of the heavenly Bridegroom he represented, he instead sought out the wife who had left him. Once she was found, he forgave her, redeemed her, brought her back to their home, and treated her as fully reconciled to himself. Hosea 3:1-2 records:

The LORD said to me, "Go, show your love to your wife again, though she is loved by another man and is an adulteress. Love her as the LORD loves the Israelites, though they turn to other gods..." So, I bought her for fifteen shekels of silver and about a homer and a lethek of barley.

Just as Hosea's actions foreshadowed, Jesus showed God's unwavering love and forgiving spirit by willingly taking a sinful but repentant people to be His Bride. By purchasing her with His blood, He lovingly reconciled us back to Himself and treats us as though we had never sinned.

THE SCARLET ROBE

In Nathaniel Hawthorne's classic novel, *The Scarlet Letter*, the main character, Hester Prynne, is charged with committing adultery. Brought out from behind prison doors, she is publicly scorned and shamed and is forced to forever wear a scarlet letter "A" on the breast of her gown.

Unwilling to reveal her lover's name, she stood alone on the platform except for the offspring of a night's passion in her arms. Hawthorne writes, "She turned her eyes downward at the scarlet letter, and even touched it with her finger, to assure herself that the infant and the shame were real. Yes! -these were her realities, -all else had vanished!"[18]

If you were made to publicly wear a scarlet letter representing your greatest failure in breaking one of God's Ten Commandments, which letter would it be?[19]

H̲aving other gods before Him
G̲raven image Idols
P̲rofaning the Lord's name
B̲reaking the Sabbath
D̲ishonoring your father and mother
M̲urder
A̲dultery

Stealing
Lying
Coveting

DO YOU HAVE YOUR LETTER? If so, slowly touch your chest one time as if you were pinning it onto yourself. Now pause for a moment. There is a weight of consequence and shame to your sin. Do you feel it?

Each broken commandment is as ugly and grotesque as the blood red animal sacrifices required under the Old Testament Mosaic law. But there is hope. His name is JESUS! Isaiah 1:18 reminds us of what He has accomplished, "'Come now, let us settle the matter,' says the LORD. 'Though your sins are like scarlet, they shall be as white as snow; though they are red as crimson, they shall be like wool.'"

Now, imagine removing your scarlet letter and pinning it onto Jesus. (Symbolically pinch it off your chest and reach up, as if pinning it on Him.)

Consider how the heavenly Bridegroom wore not just one of our scarlet letters, but an entire *robe of scarlet*.[20] This deep red robe represents every one of our filthy sins for which Jesus suffered. Isaiah 53 is painful to read, but necessary for us to better understand the depth of our Bridegroom's sacrificial love:

> *Surely He has borne our griefs and carried our sorrows; yet we esteemed Him stricken… But He was wounded for our transgressions, He was bruised for our iniquities, the chastisement for our peace was upon Him, and by his stripes we are healed. All like sheep have gone astray; We have turned, every one, to his own way; and the LORD has laid on Him the iniquity of us all. He was oppressed and He was afflicted, yet He opened not his mouth; He was led as a lamb to the slaughter, and as a*

sheep before its shearers is silent, so He opened not his mouth... For he was cut off from the land of the living. (Isaiah 53:4-7, 8b, NKJV)

Mysteriously, this unsightly story bears the good news of the Gospel! That God made Jesus who had no sin, to become sin for us, so that in Him we might become the righteousness of God.[21] Theologians call Christ's substitutionary atonement the *Great Exchange.* For it is only through Jesus that we can exchange our red, sin-stained clothes for His white robe of righteousness.

Those who put their trust in the Lamb of God will one day appear in Heaven with Him. Revelation describes that on the day when Jesus raptures His Bride-Church, there will be a great multitude that no one will be able count, from every nation, tribe, people, and language—all wearing white robes that have been washed in the blood of the Lamb.[22]

CHAPTER 2 REFLECTION

1. Leviticus 5:5 states, "When anyone becomes aware that they are guilty in any of these matters, they must confess in what way they have sinned...."

Take out a piece of paper and write down every sin that comes to mind for which you have not already repented. After you list them, humbly present each one to the Lord, asking Him to forgive you. As you do, draw a line through each one. This process may require multiple sittings.

2. Some of your sins have wounded others. James 5:16 instructs, "Therefore confess your sins to each other and pray for each other so that you may be healed. The prayer of a righteous person is powerful and effective." As the Holy Spirit leads, seek forgiveness from the one/those you have hurt and, if necessary, make appropriate restitution.

3. After you have dealt with your list of sins—destroy it! Romans 8:1-2 reminds us, "Therefore, there is now no condemnation for those who are in Christ Jesus, because through Christ Jesus the law of the Spirit who gives life has set you free from the law of sin and death." Take a moment and thank God for the freedom that is now yours!

GOD'S DIVINE SOLUTION

THE SAVIOR'S PROPOSAL

It is beyond our understanding as to why the God of the Universe desires a relationship with the likes of you and me. In truth, we all have a scarlet letter. Being omniscient, God knows exactly who we are, what we have done in the past, what we are doing in the present, and what we will do in the future. Nothing is hidden from His sight. Still, Jesus has set His heart toward us, seeing us not as who we are, but who He has destined us to be!

The heavenly Bridegroom has chosen you and courts you, not on bended knee, but with outstretched arms. You will not be forced into the relationship. You may accept His proposal of love. Or you may choose to decline it. However, He freely extends the invitation to enter an eternal union with Him, and patiently waits for your response.

For some it may come easier, having already experienced the joy of living in a safe and loving home or marriage. Others may have a tainted view of God's kind intentions by way of a painful upbringing or relationship. Regardless of your status as single or married, happy or unhappy, with Jesus every person can enter a secure and sacred bond that will endure forever with every right, privilege and blessing attached. No prenuptial agreement is asked or needed. The Lord's promise to His people stands.

OUR FREE WILL CHOICE

Everyone has been given the gift of free will to choose how to respond to the Bridegroom's proposal of love and eternal salvation. The choice is yours alone and is offered until you no longer have a heartbeat. But it is strongly recommended that you do not wait. Your life may be required of you at any moment, and your delayed response may one day become an unchangeable choice in which you will find yourself forever suffering in a fiery darkness of separation from God. Romans 6:23 offers us the choice: "For the wages of sin is death, but the gift of God is eternal life in Christ Jesus our Lord."

If your heart is stirred to commit your life to Jesus for the first time, or if you have previously done so but have turned away and feel the need to recommit, now is your opportunity! The suggested prayer below is not magical, but God will hear the sincerity of your heart. I encourage you to pray:

Heavenly Father, I thank You for loving me so much that You sent Your Son Jesus as the Way for me to receive forgiveness of sins and be released from the power of sin, Satan and death. I confess that I am a sinner. I believe that Jesus died for my sins and was raised from the dead. I no longer wish to go my own way. I renounce the works of the devil in my life. I repent and receive Jesus' perfection in exchange for my sins. I ask Jesus to come into my heart to be my Savior and Lord. I humbly ask that You fill me with Your Holy Spirit and give me power from on high to follow You all the days of my life. In Jesus' name I pray. Amen.

If you just prayed the above prayer, or your own version of it, congratulations! Welcome to the family of God! It is the single most important decision you will ever make. Heaven rejoices with you. "In the same way, I tell you, there is rejoicing in the presence of the angels of God over one sinner who repents" (Luke 15:10).

It is vital that you share your decision with other believers so they can bear witness and encourage you. Do not remain silent. Join a local Church! Seek out those with whom you can acknowledge your Savior and begin enjoying your new, dynamic relationship with Him and others. You can now rejoice and claim the praises of Isaiah 54:5, "For your Maker is your husband—the Lord Almighty is His name—the Holy One of Israel is your Redeemer; He is called the God of all the earth"

LIFTING THE VEIL OF UNBELIEF

From ancient times to modern-day, many brides walk down the aisle lightly covered with a veil. Just before she turns and comes face-to-face with her bridegroom, her father will gently lift the sheer covering away. This symbolic act represents his blessing and recognizes that there is to be no more separation between her and her bridegroom. For those who witness the unveiling, it is an endearing moment. As the Heavenly Father has led each member of the Bride-Church to His Son, we can now stand beside Him grateful that the veil of unbelief that once separated us has now been removed.

Second Corinthians 3:14-16 explains how the lifting of the spiritual veil occurs:

> ...For to this day the same veil remains when the old covenant is read. It has not been removed, because only in Christ is it taken away. Even to

this day when Moses is read, a veil covers their hearts. But whenever anyone turns to the Lord, the veil is taken away.

A NEW IDENTITY

Once Jesus' proposal of love is accepted, the dividing veil is taken away, and you are now positionally part of the Body of Christ. Ponder that for a moment. As an integral member of His Bride-Church, both individually and corporately, we can rejoice together in claiming, "I am my beloved's and my beloved is mine" (Song of Songs 6:3).

God binds us to Himself in the most beautiful of ways, including the shared name of *beloved*. It is the same name God the Father used every time He audibly spoke from Heaven regarding Jesus saying, "This is My beloved Son, in whom I am well pleased."[1]

In Greek, the word *beloved* means *esteemed, dear, favorite, worthy of love.*[2] Our new standing of worthiness before the Father is unmerited, except by the grace that's been imparted through our heavenly Bridegroom. It is essential that we humbly accept this bestowed position. Do not listen to any voice that tells you otherwise. That villainous voice is the voice of lies, who is no longer your father. In John 8:42, 44, Jesus presents the contrast between God and Satan: "'If God were your Father, you would love Me, for I have come here from God... When (the devil) lies, he speaks his native language, for he is a liar and the father of lies'" (author's parenthesis).

Therefore, if you should hear the words, "You are not loved. You are not wanted. You are a failure. You are weak. You are worthless. You will never amount to anything. Your life doesn't matter. You are stupid. You are (fill in the blank)," you now know these are not God's words. Reject these false statements and remind yourself of who you really are in Christ —*Beloved!* It is time we no longer regard ourselves or others from a worldly point of view, but instead we view ourselves and others through God's point of view.[3]

Confidently pronounce your new identity as the following:

- I am a son/daughter of God Most High.
- I am the chosen beloved of the Lord Jesus Christ.
- I am highly favored and esteemed.
- I am purchased and washed by Christ's blood.
- I am no longer condemned.
- I am clothed in the Lord Jesus' righteousness.
- I am seated with Jesus in the heavenly places.
- I am sealed and filled with the Holy Spirit of God.
- I am God's workmanship created to do good works He has prepared for me to do.

SET APART FOR CHRIST

In ancient Jewish practices, the groom would present valued gifts to his betrothed. Today an engagement ring and/or wedding band is often given, typically made of gold. Such rings serve as outward symbols of the couple's infinite love, and that the owner is set apart for another.

Although Jesus does not present the members of His Bride-Church with a physical band of gold, what we do receive is a tangible treasure nonetheless! Upon trusting in Him by faith, the abiding presence of the Holy Spirit is immediately given to indwell one's heart. Serving as a spiritual mark and seal, the Spirit will remain with us forever—as a seal of ownership upon us and a deposit guaranteeing our inheritance of what is to come.[4]

The Gospel of Luke tells us that Jesus is full of the Holy Spirit.[5] As the same Spirit abides within us, an *organic union* occurs that unites us with our heavenly Bridegroom. At times you can feel the Spirit's presence within you as your heart may pound when He prompts you to speak or do a good deed, or you may find yourself more sensitive to the things He cares about. Other times, you may receive sudden strength when you are weak, or a conviction when you sin. Just ask the Holy Spirit to show you wonderful things before you read your Bible, and watch what happens! Where there was once a hampered perception to the things of God, the Spirit opens eyes and hearts to perceive more clearly what is true. Indeed, God has made "His light shine in our hearts to give us the light of the knowledge of God's glory displayed in the face of Christ" (2 Corinthians 4:6).

SACRED LIVING TEMPLES

Just as the manifest presence of God dwelt within the physical temple in Jerusalem, the Holy Spirit resides within every believer's heart—mysteriously transforming our bodies into sacred *living temples.* First Corinthians 6:19 speaks of this transformation: "Do you not know that your bodies are temples of the Holy Spirit, who is in you, whom you have received from God?"

To understand better how our bodily tents can be living temples, we must explore the symbolic correlation to the Tent of Meeting or *tabernacle* Moses first set up in the wilderness. This would later be superseded by King Solomon's Temple built on the Temple Mount in Jerusalem. Detailed blueprints for both were given by God and had the same key elements. Both were consecrated places where the glory of the living God would come to rest.[6] Although God cannot be contained, the tabernacle and Solomon's Temple served as houses of worship where man could meet with God and seek reconciliation for sin through the sacrificial system that was temporarily set in place.

Within Moses' tabernacle and Solomon's Temple, there

were three main spaces: *Most Holy Place, Holy Place,* and the *Inner Courtyard.* A fourth *Outer Courtyard* was later incorporated. What is remarkable is how each of the three key spaces deliberately correspond to one's *spirit, soul, and body.*

The fourth space of the Outer Courtyard, represents the environmental surroundings in which a person lives. Just as the tabernacle and temple needed to be tended, so do our personal spaces. The Apostle Paul reminds us, "May God himself, the God of peace, sanctify you through and through. May your whole spirit, soul and body be kept blameless at the coming of our Lord Jesus Christ" (1 Thessalonians 5:23).

THE MOST HOLY PLACE

Of primary importance was the *Most Holy Place*, also known as the *Holy of Holies*. It contained the Ark of the Covenant where the two stone tablets of the Ten Commandments were placed inside. The Ten Commandments, being written on tablets by God himself, were brought down from Mt. Sinai by Moses. Pieces of manna and Aaron's staff were also placed inside.

On the top of the Ark of the Covenant was the *atonement cover* or Mercy Seat. The cover served as an altar where the sacrificial blood of animals would be sprinkled once a year on the Day of Atonement or *Yom Kippur* by the high priest for the forgiveness of his sins and the sins of the nation. This provisional atonement for sins foreshadowed the once and for all atonement of Christ's sacrificial blood.[7]

The Ark with its Mercy Seat stood between two winged cherubim. It was here, in the heart of the temple, where the presence of God manifested above in a cloud.[8] Both the Tabernacle and Temple served to link God's dwelling place in Heaven with man. Each also served to point towards the day when God would no longer reside in a manmade structure, but inside the most holy place of our *hearts.*[9]

The Ten Commandments placed within the Ark reflect a picture of the human heart which begin as spiritually stone-hard tablets.[10] Upon these tablets are engraved God's laws of right and wrong. It is within the chambers of the heart that life-giving oxygen is pumped into one's blood. Hearts made of stone cannot pump anything. However, once we receive Jesus and are united with the Spirit of the Living God, our spiritual *hearts of stone* are replaced with spiritual *hearts of flesh* from which Christ can then oxygenate new life into us.

Ezekiel 36:26 shares God's promise to "...give you a new heart and put a new spirit in you; I will remove from you your heart of stone and give you a heart of flesh."

THE HOLY PLACE

To gain entrance to the Most Holy Place, one must pass through the curtain or veil from within the *Holy Place*. This is the veil that was torn in two when Jesus died and gave up His spirit on the cross.[11] At that moment when the dividing barrier between a holy God and sinful humanity was removed, direct access between man and God was now available to all. Whereas the Most Holy Place symbolizes our hearts, the Holy Place is a spiritual representation of our *souls*.

The soul is the spiritual passageway into the heart. Deuteronomy 6:5 exhorts us, "You shall love the Lord your God with all your heart and with all your soul and with all your might." The Hebrew word for *soul* is defined as a person's *life, self, mind, appetite, desire, emotion, passion.*[12] It is these combined elements of your soul that make up your unique personality.

As we all have been granted free will, God does not forcibly enter a person's heart. Rather, for His Holy Spirit to come in, a person's mind must first decide, and then their will must choose to act. Emotions sometimes play into the decision, other times not, but often the emotions will follow. This explains why the battlefield for one's heart is fought in the mind. The devil ferociously fights to control our thoughts as 2 Corinthians 4:4 highlights, "...the god of this world has blinded the minds of unbelievers, so that they cannot see the light of the Gospel that displays the glory of Christ..."

There exists great imagery in the Holy Place. The Holy Place within Solomon's Temple contained the golden altar of incense, the ten gold lampstands and the ten gold tables to display the showbread. The altar of incense stood directly in front of the Ark of the Covenant, separated only by the veil. Here, incense was burned during morning and evening prayers. Prayer is a choice of the will that should engage both the mind and the Spirit—working in one accord. The Bible affirms this practice: "I will pray with my spirit, but I will also pray with my understanding; I will sing with my spirit, but I will also sing with my understanding" (1 Corinthians 14:15).

INNER COURTYARD

Outside the Holy Place was the third space of the *Inner Courtyard*. The Inner Courtyard contained the altar of burnt offering, and the bronze basin. Lavers would be added later. The Inner Court was reserved exclusively for the priests and was formed by an outer boundary wall.

Spiritually, this court represents our *physical bodies*. The bronze basin and lavers served as places of washing for the priests and animal sacrifices. We are to not only physically care for our bodies through proper hygiene but are called to offer them as *living sacrifices*. As Romans 12:1 emphasizes, "Therefore, I urge you, brothers and sisters, in view of God's mercy, to offer your bodies as a living sacrifice, holy and pleasing to God —this is your true and proper worship."

Evangelist D.L. Moody said, "The problem with a living sacrifice is that it keeps crawling off the altar." Our flesh does not like being uncomfortable, in pain, or sickly. Our flesh is also in a constant state of decline as we age—which presents various challenges. Consequently, our bodies can easily be weakened by improper hygiene or nutrition, lack of exercise or sleep, alcohol or drug abuse, sexual additions, self-inflicted harm, etc.

Additionally, there can be physical or mental disabilities that some are born with or develop later in life. Some of these disabilities are visible, but many more are invisible. If you struggle with physical or mental illness, it is wise to seek professional help and prayer. God wants you to live healthy and whole!

The battle for our minds and hearts is relentless. The devil knows if he can strategically attack any weaknesses in our flesh, he is much closer to influencing our minds and darkening our hearts. This is why it is so important to "...watch and pray so that you will not fall into temptation. The spirit is willing, but the flesh is weak" (Mark 14:38).

The key to successfully overcome the temptations of the flesh is to engage in the battle with the Word of God. Compile a list of Bible verses that you memorize or keep close at hand so that when you are tempted, frightened or hearing lying voices, you can fight back to experience relief and victory. I know from personal experience, it works!

Below are a few verses you may find helpful:

No temptation has overtaken you except what is common to mankind. And God is faithful; He will not let you be tempted beyond what you can bear. But when you are tempted, He will also provide a way out so that you can endure it. −1 Corinthians 10:13

Do not be anxious about anything, but in every situation, by prayer and petition, with thanksgiving, present your requests to God. And the peace of God, which transcends all understanding, will guard your hearts and minds in Christ Jesus. –Philippians 4:6-7

Finally, brothers and sisters, whatever is true, whatever is noble, whatever is right, whatever is pure, whatever is lovely, whatever is admirable—if anything is excellent or praiseworthy—think about such things. Whatever you have learned or received or heard from Me, or seen in Me—put it into practice. And the God of peace will be with you. – Philippians 4:8-9

For God has not given us a spirit of fear, but of power and of love and of a sound mind. –2 Timothy 1:7 (NKJV)

It is also important to watch what we allow to pass through the eye, ear, and mouth gates. What we see, hear, eat, or speak can have either a positive or negative effect. As declared in Proverbs 18:21, "The tongue has the power of life and death, and those who love it will eat its fruit."

When the wall and gates around Jerusalem were found to be in disrepair, Nehemiah acted to fortify it.[13] Just as a city could never be defended without fortified doors and locks on the gates to keep out unwanted visitors, we need to secure the entrances to our spiritual and physical doors.

OUTER COURTYARD

Lastly, there was a surrounding exterior to Moses' Tabernacle. This space would later be incorporated into Solomon's temple and named the *Outer Court(s)*. This area correlates to our physical and spiritual surroundings in which we live. Allowing unholy things into your life is dangerously harmful and greatly displeasing to God. Twice in the biblical accounts, Jesus expelled from the Temple Outer Courts the corrupt money

MARY SOLER

changers and those selling animals for sacrifice.[14] This topic will be further explored in chapter 7.

THE ALTAR OF SACRIFICE

It is no coincidence that Solomon's Temple in Jerusalem was built on the very mount where Abraham was asked by God to sacrifice his long-awaited son of promise, Isaac. The scene is recorded in Genesis when God said to Abraham, "'Take your son, your only son, whom you love—Isaac—and go to the region of Moriah. Sacrifice him there as a burnt offering on a mountain I will show you.' Early the next morning Abraham got up and loaded his donkey" (Genesis 22:2-3a).

There will come a time in every believer's life when your faith, too, will in some way be profoundly tested by God to reveal what is truly in the most holy place of your heart. Abraham was tested in the most extreme way, and yet, he obeyed God without question or delay. Venturing to where God directed, there he built an altar, bound Isaac, and even lifted the knife to slay his son. It was not until the very last moment where God showed Himself faithful, intervened, and provided a ram as a substitute for Isaac. There, Abraham sacrificed the ram as a burnt offering to God instead of his son.[15] God is seldom early, but never late.

Abraham's complete, unquestioning obedience to God was credited to him as righteousness.[16] As a result, he became known as *the father of our faith*. When our turn comes to obey, whatever it is God may ask us to do, may we too, be found faithful.

A PERSONAL ALTAR

The testing of my heart came when God asked me to lay Joseph and my marriage on the altar of sacrifice. For almost ten years I hid my sin of infidelity. However, every day as I looked in the mirror, all I saw was a "liar and a cheat." Increasingly over time God pressed upon me that I needed to tell my husband. In addition to guilt and shame, I wrestled with a great amount of fear. Fear that I would lose our marriage and destroy our three young children's world.

Ending up divorced was not something I just imagined. It was something of which I had been forewarned. Before we were married, Joseph told me at a pre-marriage conference that if I were ever unfaithful to him, it would be over. He would leave me. I remember arguing with God, trying desperately to get out of confessing my sin to my husband, but in the end, I chose to obey and face whatever consequences would come. My prayer and solace became, *"Lord, let it be enough that I obeyed You."*

JESUS AS LORD

Some of you may be familiar with the book *The Five Love Languages* by Gary Chapman.[17] Chapman describes five primary ways in which love is expressed and received. They are: *Acts of Service, Physical Touch, Gifts, Quality Time, and Words of Affirmation.* Do you know what God's love language is? In one word: Obedience. "And this is love: that we walk in obedience to His commands" (2 John 1:6).

The first most important decision you will ever make in your life is to accept the heavenly Bridegroom's proposal of love and invite Jesus into your heart to be your *Savior.* The second most important decision you will ever make is to recognize Jesus as your *Lord.* This entails stepping off the throne of your life and allowing Him to take His rightful place. As shared earlier in chapter 1, the Greek word for *lord* is defined as *he to whom a person or thing belongs, about which he has power of deciding.*[18]

Giving up control of your life takes courage and can leave you feeling frightened, insecure, even angry. I remember lifting my fist towards God and in a fit yelling, "I gave You my heart, and now You want my life?!" Anger is a common symptom of fear—fear of losing control. But honestly, how much control do any of us really have of our lives? What we can control is our responses and repentance when we fall into sin. In these pivotal moments, we must humbly and fully submit ourselves to God.

As you approach repenting of your sins and committing to live in obedience to God's Word, may you find comfort in the words of Jeremiah regarding God's intentions toward you:

"For I know the plans I have for you," declares the LORD, "plans to prosper you and not to harm you, plans to give you hope and a future. Then you will call on Me and come and pray to Me, and I will listen to you. You will seek Me and find Me when you seek Me with all your heart. I will be found by you," declares the LORD, "and will bring you back from captivity." –Jeremiah 29:11-14a

Allowing Jesus to be your *Lord* is the sure path to your best, most fulfilling life that God has planned for you. Once I repented from my sins, began yielding to the sanctifying work of the Holy Spirit, and committed to live in full obedience to God's Word, my self-centered heart slowly began to transform. I soon found myself becoming who I was truly meant to be—a vibrant member of the Body of Christ. And this can happen to you as well!

No matter what you have done, how low you have sunk, or where you are now in your life spiritually, mentally, or physically—you *can* experience a brand-new life in Christ. As 2 Corinthians 5:17 celebrates, "Therefore, if anyone is in Christ, the new creation has come: The old is gone, the new is here!" In the next four chapters, we will explore how you can cooperate to speed your transformation and ensure that you are *well prepared* for the Splendid Day of the Rapture, when the Bridegroom comes for those who belong to Him.

CHAPTER 3 REFLECTION

1. Is Jesus your Savior? If so, have you shared your decision with another believer?

2. Do you sense the presence of God's Holy Spirit within you? In what ways?

3. Have you ever had to put someone or something on the *altar of sacrifice?* What happened? What lessons did you learn through that experience?

4. If you have never intentionally told Jesus you would like to grant Him *Lordship* over your life, take some time to do so now.

PART 2: HOW YOU CAN PREPARE

LOOK IN THE MIRROR

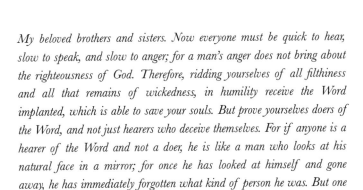

My beloved brothers and sisters. Now everyone must be quick to hear, slow to speak, and slow to anger; for a man's anger does not bring about the righteousness of God. Therefore, ridding yourselves of all filthiness and all that remains of wickedness, in humility receive the Word implanted, which is able to save your souls. But prove yourselves doers of the Word, and not just hearers who deceive themselves. For if anyone is a hearer of the Word and not a doer, he is like a man who looks at his natural face in a mirror; for once he has looked at himself and gone away, he has immediately forgotten what kind of person he was. But one who has looked intently at the perfect law, the law of freedom, and has continued in it, not having become a forgetful hearer but an active doer, this person will be blessed in what he does. – James 1:19-25 NASB

A ROYAL MESS

As I have shared portions of my life testimony, it's obviously not all pretty. But my biggest fall came *after* I prayed to receive Jesus as my Savior. Did you hear that? My worst sin was committed after I became a believer, not before. So much for representing the heavenly Bridegroom or His

Bride-Church well. At that time in my life, I was behaving like a hypocrite—calling myself a Christ follower, but acting far different. So was I a saved, born-again believer? Yes, because when Jesus redeemed me, it was complete. His blood atoned for all my past, present and future sins.[1] But I was a mess—certainly not a holy, radiant bride of Christ.

Sadly, this is the state of many in the Church today. Many individuals are living a life incompatible with the teachings of the Bible. This is not my judgment, but the assessment of Jesus as seen in His address to five of His seven churches in Revelation 2:1-3:22. *This translates to mean that over 71 percent of the global church is not ready to meet the Savior.*

Each of the seven churches Jesus identifies represent spiritual categories of believers and congregations that exist around the world throughout the ages—from the early church to today. All seven are recognized by Jesus as His lampstands and bearing His witness to the world, however five of them have serious sins taking place within them for which repentance is needed.

Interestingly, within every church there exists three types of people:

1. Those who are true believers in Christ and are walking faithfully, not perfect—but faithfully, before God. They will be raptured to Heaven on the Splendid Day and richly rewarded when Jesus returns.

2. Those who are true believers in Christ and need to turn away from a hypocritical mindset and/or lifestyle. They will be raptured to Heaven on the Splendid Day when Jesus comes—but miss out on eternal rewards.

3. Those who are *counterfeit* believers—also known as *weeds* or *tares*. They appear to belong to the Bride-

Church but are of the unredeemed. Unless they
repent and receive Jesus by faith into their hearts,
they will miss the Rapture.

It is important we look at the five compromised churches
Jesus addresses, because "Bad company corrupts good character."[2] The first church of Ephesus has become so caught up in
their works that they have forgotten their first love—Jesus. The
second church of Pergamum has allowed Satan to set up his
throne in their midst and have been led into idolatry and
sexual immorality.

The third church of Thyatira allows sexually immoral
teachings and practices. The fourth church of Sardis is
described as almost spiritually dead. The fifth church of
Laodicea is lukewarm in their faith and has shut Jesus out—
needing to open the door to fellowship once again. To those
who Jesus calls out but do not repent, there will be consequences. However, to all who *repent and overcome*, they are
promised to be rewarded.

In contrast, two of the seven churches are fully
commended by Jesus. In word and deed, they both prove themselves as faithful. The first church of Smyrna has the high
honor of suffering persecution—even death—for Jesus' name-
sake and will be abundantly rewarded. While the other faithful
church of Philadelphia will also patiently endure persecution
and not deny Jesus' name. She will be rewarded by being *kept*
"from the hour of trial that is going to come on the whole
world" (Revelation 3:10b). *Kept* from the coming trials of this
world. Think about that. This is the group, I imagine, many
believers would want to align themselves with. I certainly do.

While these churches may have names unfamiliar to you,
the spiritual condition of each group is a direct indicator of
their level of preparedness for the Splendid Day of the
Rapture. Which group do you think you currently align? If you

would like to do more research, you can read Jesus' complete sermon to the seven churches in Revelation 2:1-3:22. There is also a summary provided in Appendix A at the end of this book. Ultimately, the real question is: How will you look on the day Jesus comes for you?

I ONCE HEARD Coach Bill McCartney speak at Calvary Community Church in Westlake Village, California. He retold a shocking wedding scene as described by author Nancy DeMoss Wolgemuth. The story is transcribed below:

> *Imagine with me for a moment a Royal Wedding. The invitations have been sent out, all the preparations have been made, the guests have arrived, the music is playing, the flowers are beautiful, and the auditorium is decked for a king and queen. The bridegroom and his attendants come to the front of the auditorium, and the wedding march begins to play. We all arise. We're sitting toward the front. It's a little hard for us to see the back, but we get a glimpse of the bride beginning to come down the aisle toward her bridegroom. We crane our necks to see the bride, and as she gets closer, it looks like something is wrong.*
>
> *It can't be, but yes! Her veil is torn and ripped! It's askew on her head. She gets closer, and we see that her dress is wrinkled. It looks like it's been stuffed in a box for weeks. As she walks by the aisle where we're sitting, we see that it's not even white anymore. It's soiled. It's stained. It's torn. Her hair is in disarray! She has no makeup. Her face is filthy. She has dirt smudges on her arms, and we say, "We've never seen anything like this before!"*
>
> *Then our eyes turn as she approaches her bridegroom, and we see the look of unbelievable sorrow in his eyes as he realizes that his bride did not care enough to get ready for the wedding.*[3]

Iᴛ's hard to imagine a bride presenting herself on her wedding day covered in such filth and disarray. And yet, this is the picture Jesus' paints of most of the members of His church in Revelation prior to the Rapture. If action is not taken to prepare, many may find themselves left behind, panicked, bewildered, and wondering why. But take heart, this potentially disastrous situation *can be avoided.* It's time to get ready for *our* Royal Wedding Day!

PREPARING FOR OUR ROYAL WEDDING DAY

Nothing captures the world's attention quite like a royal wedding. People from virtually every country on the planet tune in to watch the beauty, tradition, spectacle and grandeur of the ceremony and celebration on a level that few can experience personally. In viewing such an event from the comfort of our living room sofas, it allows us an opportunity to fantasize what it would be like to have such a fairy tale dream come true in our own lives.

Some may remember the wedding of the heir to the British throne, Charles, Prince of Wales to Lady Diana Spencer in 1981 at St. Paul's Cathedral. It was billed as the *wedding of the century* and was watched by a global TV audience of 750 million people. Thirty years later, their older son Prince William, Duke of Cambridge married Catherine (Kate) Middleton in 2011 at Westminster Abbey. The occasion was declared an official public holiday in the United Kingdom.

Many Disney movies have exploded with success over the years simply by presenting this widely popular royal wedding theme by artfully changing the characters, time periods and locations. Whether in a real or fantasy world, we just can't seem to get enough of it.

But wait! There is coming an unprecedented Royal Wedding that will infinitely surpass anything the world has ever seen. The marvelous news is that we are not only invited to attend the exclusive occasion in person, but as the global Church, we have been chosen to stand beside the Royal Bridegroom Himself as His radiant Bride. Knowing what we have to look forward to, how do we prepare in practical ways for our grand destiny? Let's take a look.

BE BAPTIZED

The first righteous act of preparation every believer is called to do is to be *baptized*. According to Hebrew tradition, a few days before a wedding both bride and groom would prepare themselves individually by taking a water immersion bath called a *mikveh*. This symbolized spiritual cleansing.

Being sinless, Jesus did not need a mikveh, but as the heavenly Bridegroom, He prepared Himself in this way for His Bride-Church in order to meet the requirements of the Hebrew law. In Matthew 3:13-15, Christ's preparation is recorded:

> *Then Jesus came from Galilee to the Jordan to be baptized by John. But John tried to deter Him, saying, "I need to be baptized by You, and do You come to me?" Jesus replied, "Let it be so now; it is proper for us to do this to fulfill all righteousness." Then John consented.*

Likewise, baptism is a first step of obedience that every member of Jesus' Bride-Church is to follow.

After I submitted to Jesus as my Lord, I began to grow in my love and knowledge of Him through weekly Bible study. In time, the importance of water baptism was highlighted to me. My parents baptized me as an infant. I remain grateful and continue to honor their act of faith to publicly dedicate me to

God at a young age, raise me in the church and instill in me Christian values. Many of you, too, may have already been baptized or dedicated as infants.

However, desiring to follow in Jesus' footsteps, I was compelled by the Holy Spirit to be baptized of my own free will. This was in no way to disregard what my parents had previously done. Even Jesus Himself was brought to the temple by His parents and consecrated to God as an infant and then later was baptized as an adult.[4]

I did this through an event at our church, Calvary Chapel of South Bay, arranged at Cabrillo Beach in San Pedro, California in 1987. Baptized in the name of the Father, Son, and Holy Spirit, I momentarily went down into the water, symbolizing my death to self and sin, and then came back up to the surface, spiritually resurrected to new life with Christ.[5] Feeling reborn and clean, the day of my adult baptism was one of the most joyous days of my life!

Baptism does not save us (consider the repentant thief on the cross who was promised to go directly with Jesus into paradise),[6] but baptism does serve as a sign of spiritual cleansing and rebirth and should be an individual's first public act of obedience after receiving salvation. It is often referred to as *believer's baptism*. I waited several years into adulthood to take this step but was so grateful when I finally did. My baptism was a turning point—where I fully submitted myself to the Lord.

Some of you may have already been baptized independently of what your parents did or did not do for you. I rejoice with you! However, if you were baptized because you were pressured or felt you needed to check some religious box, I encourage you to pray about being baptized again. God sees and cares most about your heart. Baptism is only counted as a righteous act if it comes out of a heart of love and devotion for the heavenly Bridegroom. It is an action where you intentionally remove your old stained, soiled clothes of sin, and put on the new righteous robe of Christ as described in Galatians 3:27, "...for all of you who were baptized into Christ have clothed yourselves with Christ."

For those of you who were once baptized of your own choice and with pure motives but have since stumbled or walked away from your relationship with Jesus, it is not necessary for you to be baptized again. All that is needed is sincere, humble confession and repentance before the Lord. Our Savior always stands ready to clean us up. Jesus told His disciples on the night He washed their feet, "Those who have had a bath need only to wash their feet; their whole body is clean" (John 13:10).

For those of you who have never been baptized and desire to be obedient in taking this important first step, may the exhortation of Acts 22:16 motivate you to act: "Now what are you waiting for? Get up, be baptized and wash your sins away, calling on His name."

BE SANCTIFIED

The second righteous act members of the Bride-Church must submit to is the process of *sanctification*. Unger's Bible Dictionary defines sanctification as *separation from the secular and sinful and setting apart for a sacred purpose.* As living temples of Christ's Spirit, the sanctification process cleanses our spirit, soul, and body so that we can truly experience renewed freedom in Christ.

A transformation is necessary so we can think and act in a godly manner, and more accurately reflect our heavenly Bridegroom to others. This involves actively driving out any known sin as directed in Luke 11:35-36, "See to it, then, that the light within you is not darkness. Therefore, if your whole body is full of light, and no part of it dark, it will be just as full of light as when a lamp shines its light on you."

Sanctification is something we are incapable of doing on our own. It is a work of the Holy Spirit who will systematically lead you. As darkness loses its place within us, it allows us to experience more of Christ's presence, power, and purpose in our lives. In Psalm 139:24, we are provided an effective prayer: "See if there is any offensive way in me, and lead me in the way everlasting."

In his book *The Holy Spirit: Activating God's Power in Your Life*,[7] Dr. Billy Graham explained that we must "deal honestly and completely with every known sin... We must not be content with a casual examination of our lives... We must confess not only what we think is sin, but what the Holy Spirit labels as sin when we really listen to His voice from the Word of God."

Colossians 3:5-10 provides a list of sins that must be rooted out of our lives:

> *Put to death, therefore, whatever belongs to your earthly nature: sexual immorality, impurity, lust, evil desires and greed, which is idolatry. Because of these, the wrath of God is coming. You used to walk in these ways, in the life you once lived. But now you must also rid yourselves of all such things as these: anger, rage, malice, slander, and filthy language from your lips. Do not lie to each other, since you have taken off your old self with its practices and have put on the new self, which is being renewed in knowledge in the image of its Creator.*

As we work with the Holy Spirit to rid our hearts of sin, sanctification takes place. This purification is necessary for us to ready ourselves as members of the spotless Bride-Church. Let's next look closely at the different *types* of sin.

LIFTING THE VEIL OF SINS, TRANSGRESSIONS, AND INIQUITIES

A dividing curtain or *veil of separation* exists between fallen man and a holy God. King David felt this separation after he committed adultery with Bathsheba, and then compounded his sin by having her husband, Uriah, murdered.[8] David did not immediately repent, but after a year of wrestling with feelings of guilt, he finally approached God for pardon. His petition is recorded in Psalm 51:1-2, 4,10-11:

> *Have mercy on me, O God, according to your unfailing love; according to your great compassion blot out my transgressions. Wash away all my iniquity and cleanse me from my sin... Against you, you only, have I sinned and done what is evil in your sight... Create in me a pure heart, O God, and renew a steadfast spirit within me. Do not cast me from your presence or take your Holy Spirit from me...*

In David's confession he uses three distinct terms: *sin, transgressions,* and *iniquity.* On a basic level, each term describes a category of missing God's mark of holiness and perfection. This is something for which every person is guilty. Romans 3:23 reminds us that "All have sinned and fall short of the glory of God."

However, in seeking forgiveness, it is important to be specific in confessing the wrongdoing. As David modeled, each sin fits under one of the three categories and must be appropriately addressed. A general request such as "God, forgive me for all of my sins," falls short of true humility in allowing the Holy Spirit to thoroughly search your heart and bring awareness to the areas where He desires to clean, heal, and transform.

It is helpful to understand these categories of sin so you can be effective in confessing them. God always stands ready to forgive! "The LORD, the LORD God, merciful and gracious, longsuffering, and abounding in goodness and truth, keeping mercy for thousands, forgiving iniquity and transgression and sin" (Exodus 34:6-7 NKJV).

UNDERSTANDING SIN

The New Unger's Bible Dictionary defines *sin* as *a falling away from or missing the right path.* We sin when we *think* sexually immoral thoughts and when we entertain impurity, evil intent, hatred, selfish ambition, malice, deceit, hypocrisy, hatred, bitterness, unrighteous anger, jealousy, envy, or lust.[9] Sin starts in our thought life.

We also sin when we set up *idols in our hearts.* An idol is more than an image of a deity. An idol can be anything, person, pursuit, or pleasure that we give admiration, adoration, or devotion to with a commitment or intensity above God. In Ezekiel 14, the Lord rebuked the Israelites for defiling themselves by setting up idols in their hearts, which put a stumbling block between them and God.

We may not act upon our wicked thoughts or inclinations, but the Lord knows what they are and calls them sin. While we may hide our thoughts and inner attitudes from other people, we can't hide them from God who "searches every heart and understands every desire and every thought" (1 Chronicles 28:9b).

Unforgiveness is another sin that can be harbored in our hearts. Jesus made it clear: "But if you do not forgive others their sins, your Father will not forgive your sins" (Matthew 6:15). One of the most effective ways to forgive another person who has wounded you is to pray for them. As recorded in Luke 23:34, Jesus set an example by praying for all while He hung on the cross: "Father, forgive them, for they do not know what they are doing."

The sin of unforgiveness will be further explored in chapter 5.

UNDERSTANDING TRANSGRESSION

Sometimes we take sinful thoughts and attitudes a step further and *transgress*. Transgress means to *violate a law, command or moral code; to pass over or go beyond a limit or boundary.*[10] We step over the line when we act upon our wretched thoughts. When a crime takes place, a transgression has occurred.

On Calvary, there were two thieves who were being punished for crimes they had carried out. Crucified between them was Jesus. Jesus committed no crime and was innocent, but He was put to death for our violations and was therefore "numbered with the transgressors" (Mark 15:28).

UNDERSTANDING INIQUITY

Iniquity is most often associated with generational sins and repeated patterns of transgression. One definition of iniquity is *perversity, depravity, anything unjustly acquired.*[11] Each generation has the moral duty to protect their ancestry. Whenever someone sins or transgresses, it can provide an opening for the devil to continue his destructive work in the next generation of a family. Iniquities can pass down through a bloodline or spiritual covering, such as grandparents, parents, or guardians.

Iniquities will sometimes skip a generation and be imposed upon the next. Generational iniquity is a reality that is highlighted in Exodus 34:6-7:

> *The LORD, the LORD, the compassionate and gracious God, slow to anger, abounding in love and faithfulness, maintaining love to thousands, and forgiving wickedness, rebellion and sin. Yet He does not leave the*

guilty unpunished; He punishes the children and their children for the sin of the parents to the third and fourth generation.

Although God does not hold children accountable for the sins of their fathers, the devil is a schemer and may try to tempt or oppress a current generation with some transgression from the past that was never repented of by a prior generation. Examples of these are alcoholism, drug abuse, sexual abuse, practices of witchcraft, or the occult.

If you are aware of such things in your family history, as a believer you can bring the iniquity before God and ask Him to forgive and cancel the specific family iniquity by the name of the Lord Jesus Christ and through the power of His blood.

The action to seek generational forgiveness is presented in Nehemiah 9:2 where "Those of Israelite descent had separated themselves from all foreigners. They stood in their places and confessed their sins and the sins of their ancestors."

With great intentionality, Joseph and I invited the Holy Spirit to reveal our individual and familial sins, transgressions, and iniquities of past generations so they could be properly dealt with. Breaking off our own sin and generational curses was a process that took several years. Each time something ungodly was exposed and repented of, we experienced greater freedom and relief from oppressive forces that had existed over our family.

We give all praise to God—our strong Deliverer! How liberating it is to know that "...as far as the east is from the west, so far has He removed our transgressions from us" (Psalm 103:12).

Purpose to end current and generational sins with you! Your life and family no longer need to be held hostage by the enemy.[12] Jesus desires His Bride-Church to be completely set free so that evil no longer has authority nor place to attack.

On the cross, Jesus secured victory over darkness, but we

have the responsibility to apply His triumph to our own lives. *If not you, who? If not now, when?* Once the darkness is chased out, you will find more room within your heart and life for Christ's love and light to shine through!

MAJOR HINDRANCES—GUILT, CONDEMNATION AND SHAME

As you allow the Holy Spirit to lead you through the process of sanctification as described above, there may be associations to sin that can become hindrances to experiencing total freedom in Christ. Three of the common hindrances are: Guilt, Condemnation and Shame.

GUILT

Guilt, conviction, or remorse are natural feelings we have when we sin. These emotions are healthy evidence that you recognize that you have committed an offense against God by breaking one or more of His commands. God's law is written on every human heart and provides an inherent compass to help us discern between right and wrong.[13] We all sin at different times and feel the weight of conviction. However, what we do with that feeling can be the difference between life and death.

Sadly, Judas Iscariot provides an example of guilt that resulted in death. Matthew 27:3-5 records his tragic end:

> *When Judas, who had betrayed Him, saw that Jesus was condemned, he was seized with remorse and returned the thirty silver coins to the chief priests and the elders. "I have sinned," he said, "for I have betrayed innocent blood." "What is that to us" they replied. "That is*

your responsibility." So, Judas threw the money into the temple and left.
Then he went away and hanged himself.

Judas was sorrowful for what he had done, but he did not repent of his sin nor put his trust in Jesus who could save. Judas was without excuse. As one of the 12 disciples, Judas directly heard Jesus' teachings and was eyewitness to countless miracles, signs, and wonders. Still, it is not recorded that Judas ever called Jesus "Lord." Instead, his trust was in the world. Unwilling to take hold of the hope Jesus extended, Judas saw no option but to end his life. This truth is seen in 2 Corinthians 7:10, "Godly sorrow brings repentance that leads to salvation and leaves no regret, but worldly sorrow brings death."

Compare Judas' story to Peter's. Peter also sinned against Jesus. He denied Him three times.[14] However, unlike Judas, Peter was guilt-ridden with godly sorrow and chose to trust the One who he knew could save his soul.[15] Furthermore, it is recorded that Peter called Jesus *Lord* over 20 times in the New Testament, reflecting the presence of the Holy Spirit in his life: "No one can say, 'Jesus is Lord,' except by the Holy Spirit" (1 Corinthians 12:3b). No matter how deep your sin, expressing godly sorrow and choosing to trust Jesus Christ restores you to a right relationship with God and an abundant life!

CONDEMNATION

Once forgiven by God, you no longer stand condemned. Your guilt is removed. Therefore, if you continue to hear an accusing voice, it's important to discern the source. Is it yours or the devil's? If you assess the voice is from the devil, remind yourself that Satan, "the accuser of our brothers and sisters, who accuses them before our God day and night, has been hurled down" (Revelation 12:10). Christ won the battle; however, the devil's strategy is to get us preoccupied with our past failures. It is time to stop looking in the rearview mirror and *forgive yourself.* God certainly has.

Sometimes you may be pressured into feeling guilty over things for which you are innocent. *False guilt* can try to impose itself upon you. Ask the Holy Spirit to search your heart and show you if there is any substance to the accusation. If not, reject it and declare Romans 8:1-2 out loud: "Therefore, there is now no condemnation for those who are in Christ Jesus, because through Christ Jesus the law of the Spirit who gives life has set you free from the law of sin and death."

SHAME

The definition of *shame* is *a painful feeling of consciousness of something dishonorable, improper, or ridiculous done by oneself or another.* Shame comes upon us and makes us feel awful because of sinful or embarrassing things we have done. Daniel 9:7-8 makes the connection, "Lord, You are righteous, but this day we are covered with shame... because of our unfaithfulness to You."

Shame also comes upon a person because of hurtful things that were done to them. Sometimes it can take years for those who have been sexually abused to speak of what happened so they can begin to heal. Job, who was attacked by Satan, said, "If I am guilty—woe to me! Even if I am innocent, I cannot lift my head, for I am full of shame and drowned in my affliction" (Job 10:15).

Shame is tied very closely to fear of what people would think about you. Shockingly, some people feel no shame at all nor care about what people may think of them. Their hearts have become callous and dangerously far from God. The more they sin and fall for the lie that they've done nothing wrong, the more insensitive and hardened their hearts become. Jeremiah describes their reprehensible state: "Are they ashamed of their detestable conduct? No, they have no shame at all; they do not even know how to blush. So they will fall among the fallen; they will be brought down when I punish them," says the LORD" (Jeremiah 6:15).[16]

Although God desires that every person turn from their wicked ways and live, He will not let the unrepentant go unpunished. For some, it is the sting of discipline that will awaken a person to their sin and shame. Paul guided the Corinthian church in how to deal with a member who had fallen into perversion. Paul said, "hand this man over to Satan for the destruction of the flesh, so that his spirit may be saved on the day of the Lord" (1 Corinthians 5:5). While this may sound harsh, God's goal is for the wayward believer to repent and turn back to Him.

LIFTING THE VEIL OF SHAME

Shame produces a veil that causes us to hide from others so we can avoid full disclosure. Shame deceives others and works to steal our joy and identity as beloved children of God and Jesus' cherished one.

We see this dramatically illustrated in Genesis, where on Jacob's wedding night, Leah's identity was literally veiled from Jacob. He thought the bride with whom he shared his wedding bed was Leah's sister, Rachel. However, upon waking up the next morning, Jacob discovered the intimacy he shared was based on a lie.[17] This is how shame works. It causes us to mask ourselves from others, fearing we would be rejected if it becomes known who we really are.

True intimacy is based on honesty. Leah's father, Laban, put her up to the task of deceiving Jacob, and Leah played along out of fear. She was described as having "weak eyes," while her sister Rachel was said to be "lovely in form and beauty."[18] Because of this, all through Leah's wedding night not one word did she utter for fear that Jacob would recognize her voice. The poor fellow knew nothing of who he was lying with until the morning sun revealed the truth! Truth always has a way of being brought into the light.

Although Leah's father was a trickster, there is another father who tries to lead *us* down a deceptive road. He is Satan, a liar, and the father of lies,[19] who tempts us to keep our mouths shut. He knows that once our sin and shame is revealed, he will lose his power over us. The question that must be asked is *Who is your father?* Is it God—the father of all truth? Or is it Satan—the father of all lies? Is there a lie or sin that the devil has told you to keep quiet about? Are you complying? Beware!

I was silent about my sin, and consequently, I wore shame as a garment for way too long. In shame, I tried to hide my sin from my husband, but that was not the way I was intended to live, nor are you. Jesus wants us to understand that on the cross, He dealt not only with our sin, but also our shame—scorning it![20] It was not until I was honest with Joseph and, in time, my family—that the veil was lifted, and I was completely set free from shame and the influence of the devil. It is why I can publicly share my story today.

Some of you may be walking around with a veil of shame shrouding you. But God wants you to live in lasting freedom from shame's influence. It is time to allow your true Father, who is in Heaven, to lift your veil and cast it away forever! "Those who look to Him are radiant; their faces are never covered with shame" (Psalm 34:5).

A TRANSFORMED LIFE

In the Gospel of John there is an account of Jesus meeting a Samaritan woman. The Samaritans were despised by the Jewish people. They were considered as half-breeds of corrupted Israelites who defiled themselves with pagans. Not only was this woman a Samaritan, but she also lived an immoral life.

Existing in the shadows, she would intentionally go to draw water from the town well during the heat of the day to avoid the scorn-filled looks of others. The Samaritan woman with whom Jesus encountered by the well, wore a heavily cloaked veil of shame. Her past consisted of five failed marriages, and the man she currently lived with was not her husband. Who would want anything to do with *her*? Jesus would.

There by the well He waited. When the woman arrived, Jesus engaged her by asking for a drink. Bewildered that a Jewish man would ask a drink from a Samaritan woman, she asked Him how He could do such a thing? Jesus' response was to tell her of the living water He gives that springs up into everlasting life.

"Sir, give me this water," she implored, "that I may not thirst, nor come here to draw."

Jesus' reply was to ask her to call her *husband*. Admitting that she had no husband, Jesus acknowledged that she spoke truthfully, and that she also has had five husbands, and the man she was now with was not her husband. Her shame was now unveiled, but curiously—she did not feel condemned, nor did she run away.

Recognizing Jesus was a prophet, she questioned Him about the proper place of worship. Was it the mountain where the Samaritans worship or in Jerusalem—where the Jews worship? Jesus answered that it is not the location of worship that matters, but that the Father seeks worshippers who worship in spirit and truth. Not fully understanding, the woman attempts to conclude the discussion by saying that when Messiah comes, He will explain everything. What happened next was unprecedented—as Jesus reveals for the first time that *He* is the long-awaited Messiah!

And so, it was the Father's will that this half Jewish, half Gentile, sinful person would be the first one to be introduced to the *Eternal Husband!*[21] The story of the Samaritan woman at the well is a portrait of the *one new man* Paul spoke about in Ephesians 2:14-15, where worshippers will be made up of both Jew and Gentile—reconciled to God as one body through the cross. Together they will one day drink from the heavenly streams of living water.[22]

As the woman put her faith in Jesus, she did not allow her past life of sin to keep the good news of Messiah to herself. No! She physically (and spiritually) left her water jug behind and ran back to the village to evangelize. Because of what Jesus did for her, many came to also believe.[23] There is power in a testimony. Don't be afraid to share yours!

CHAPTER 4 REFLECTION

1. What do you see when you look in the mirror? A man or woman of compromise or a sanctified saint?

2. In following Jesus' example, have you been baptized? If you have not yet taken this important step, begin to make plans to be baptized soon!

3. Understanding the difference between sin, transgression, and iniquity, is there any additional work of repentance you need to do to fully set yourself and/or family lines free? Take some time to confess to the Lord, thanking Him for His love and forgiveness.

4. Do you feel veiled in shame for things you have done? On the cross, Jesus took both your sin and shame upon Himself. Own your sin, repent from it, and choose to no longer allow it to have power over you.

5. God wants to use your story. If you have never done so, take time to write out your testimony. Include what your life was like before Jesus, describe your turning point, the difference it made, and where you are now on your life journey with Him. Keep it simple. As doors open for you to share, the version or length of your story will vary depending on your audience or circumstance.

TAKE A CLOSER LOOK

INSIGHTS FROM JOSEPH SOLER

They made the bronze basin and its bronze stand from the mirrors of the women who served at the entrance to the Tent of Meeting. – Exodus 38:8

In taking an honest look at ourselves in the mirror, some of our dirt smudges are easier to see—while others are not so obvious. Unforgiveness is one of them, as it is not so self-evident a sin. We may reason that we are justified in harboring unforgiveness. However, unforgiveness is a blind spot. Blind spots are dangerous and must be removed. 1 John 2:9-11 points this out:

> *Anyone who claims to be in the light but hates a brother or sister is still in the darkness. Anyone who loves their brother and sister lives in the light, and there is nothing in them to make them stumble. But whoever hates a brother or sister is in the darkness and walks around in the*

darkness. They do not know where they are going, because the darkness has blinded them.

Jesus emphasizes that one of His purposes for coming into the world was to bring sight to the blind, both physically *and* spiritually.

Jesus said, "For judgment I have come into this world, so that the blind will see and those who see will become blind." Some Pharisees who were with Him heard Him say this and asked, "What? Are we blind too?" Jesus said, "If you were blind, you would not be guilty of sin; but now that you claim that you see, your guilt remains." —John 9:39-41

The Institute for Family Studies published an article in January 2018 which stated that the concept of forgiveness is a very interesting thing. Everyone desires to be forgiven, but most people have difficulty forgiving others. I know this well from my own experience.

LIFTING THE VEIL OF UNFORGIVENESS

At age 36, I was a happy man. I had been married to Mary, the love of my life for fourteen years. We shared three beautiful children under the age of ten. My career was on the fast track, and we had just bought a nice house in a great neighborhood. Life was good. However, all that changed one night.

At that time in our lives, Mary worked as an adjunct professor at a nearby community college. She taught evening classes so that I could take care of the children while she worked. One night, she was over two hours late in getting home. I was extremely concerned but had no way to contact her to make sure she was safe, as this was before we had cell phones.

Mary finally arrived home around 11:00 p.m. I was

relieved that she was home, but also concerned about what happened that made her late. When she walked through the door, Mary was pale and appeared shaken. Before I could ask if she was OK, she said, "We need to talk."

With tears in her eyes, she told me she was late because she had sat in her car for a couple of hours in the college parking lot after class, wrestling with God. She said that the Holy Spirit pressed her to reveal to me a secret that she had sworn she would take to her grave. In obedience to God, she confessed that she had been unfaithful to me ten years earlier. She told me that she had repented before the Lord but vowed to never tell me.

Mary was rightly afraid that the confession would bring an end to our marriage. Fourteen years earlier in our pre-marriage church course, one of the topics the leaders had us discuss was infidelity and how we would handle it if it occurred. My exact words to Mary during that exercise were, "I will divorce you if you cheat on me."

In now confessing her failure to me, Mary knew she was placing our marriage on the altar of sacrifice and would have to live with the consequences that might follow. Nevertheless, by this time in her life, it was more important for her to obey God than to try to preserve our marriage by continuing to cover up her sin.

As I listened to her confession, I was stunned, sick to my stomach, and unable to speak. I had faced many difficult things in my life, but this was the worst. It shook me to the core. Although I had been a believer for 12 years, studied God's Word faithfully and even led a Bible study, I was not prepared to handle this news. At least not God's way. God's way is clear. Jesus said in Matthew 6:15, "If you do not forgive others their sins, your Father will not forgive your sins." Jesus illustrated this truth in the parable of the unmerciful servant.

PARABLE OF THE UNMERCIFUL SERVANT

Therefore, the kingdom of Heaven is like a king who wanted to settle accounts with his servants. As he began... a man who owed him ten thousand bags of gold was brought to him. Since he was not able to pay, the master ordered that he and his wife and his children and all that he had be sold to repay the debt.

At this the servant fell on his knees before him. "Be patient with me," he begged, "and I will pay back everything." The servant's master took pity on him, canceled the debt and let him go.

But when that servant went out, he found one of his fellow servants who owed him a hundred silver coins. He grabbed him and began to choke him. "Pay back what you owe me!" he demanded.

His fellow servant fell to his knees and begged him, "Be patient with me, and I will pay it back."

But he refused. Instead, he went off and had the man thrown into prison until he could pay the debt. When the other servants saw what had happened, they were outraged and went and told their master... Then the master called the servant in. "You wicked servant," he said, "I canceled all that debt of yours because you begged me to. Shouldn't you have had mercy on your fellow servant just as I had on you?" In anger his master handed him over to the jailers to be tortured, until he should pay back all he owed.

This is how my Heavenly Father will treat each of you unless you forgive your brother or sister from your heart. —Matthew 18:23-35

As I look back at my actions, I realize now that I fit the description of the wicked servant. I knew I was supposed to forgive my wife because God forgave me, but I found it too difficult to do. My pride was deeply wounded, and my thoughts about her offense were caught in a loop. I repeatedly asked myself, "How could she have done this to me? I am a good husband, a man of integrity." But that was not the whole truth.

I, too, had sin. I kept looking at *the speck* in Mary's eye, while ignoring *the plank* in my own eye.[1]

The truth was that I struggled with pornography. Early in our marriage I bought into the lie that there was no harm in looking at graphic sexual images, and so I brought pornographic magazines into our bedroom "to spice things up." I quickly became addicted and continued to view pornography on my own intermittently for more than ten years when away from home on business trips. I lusted in my heart after the women in the magazines and videos, fantasizing about participation in the vile things portrayed in them. Jesus said that lust of the heart is the same as adultery.[2]

I came to recognize that viewing pornography made me an adulterer too. Convicted of this sin, I repented before God and took the necessary steps to remove and avoid all pornography. Unjustly, however, I remained unwilling to extend Mary the same grace and forgiveness that God had shown me.

HOLDING ON TO A ROCK

In the story of the woman caught in adultery told in John 8:1-11, Jesus skillfully caused the crowd to reflect on their own sin. As the accusers each held onto a rock ready to stone the woman to death as the law requires, Jesus bent down and began writing on the ground with His finger. As they questioned Him, He straightened up and said,

> *"Let any one of you who is without sin be the first to throw the stone at her." Again He stooped to the ground and wrote. At this, those who heard began to go away one at a time, the older ones first, until only Jesus was left, with the woman still standing there. Jesus straightened up and asked her, "Woman, where are they? Has no one condemned you?" "No one, sir," she said. "Then neither do I condemn you," Jesus declared. "Go now and leave your life of sin."* –John 8:7b-11

As a result of personal introspection, every accuser dropped the physical *rock of judgment* they had been clenching in their hands and quietly chose to walk away. I knew that forgiving Mary was the right response, but it was something I was not yet ready to do. Instead, I chose to hold onto my rock of judgment. For many years, I wanted to throw that rock at Mary, time and time again.

You may be holding onto a rock of judgment that you have not been willing to drop. You deeply desire to pummel someone. Perhaps it is your spouse who was, or is, being unfaithful to you. Or maybe it's another person in your life who betrayed, abused, neglected, or mistreated you. Regardless of the person or the offense, Christ calls you to forgive.

In the case of infidelity, God does provide divorce as a biblical way out. However, His desire is for reconciliation. That said, God does not require anyone to remain in an abusive marriage. If this is your situation, you may need to separate from your spouse. You may also need to seek legal protection and pastoral support. God loves you and always wants you and your children to be safe.

Whether we remain in relationship or not, it is only when we have the heart of Christ and can see our offender through His eyes, that we are able to extend forgiveness. Some may choose to remain in the relationship. Jesus was the only one who stayed with the woman caught in adultery after her accusers left. He remained out of love, compassion, and forgiveness for her. Being sinless, Jesus was the only one who could have justly thrown a rock, but He did not even pick one up. Instead, He exhorted the woman to "go and sin no more."

My motives for staying in our marriage were not as pure. Rather than forgive Mary, as Jesus modeled, I chose to remain to avoid the impact a divorce would have on our kids, finances, families, and friendships. This attitude was wrong and caused much suffering for Mary, our children and me. So, there I was, a mess in every respect.

THE 3 STAGES OF UNFORGIVENESS

My emotions took me through 3 different stages:

Numbness came first and lasted several days after hearing Mary's confession. I could not believe that the woman I loved would do such a thing. At times I was in denial mode, pretending that the betrayal never happened, but more often I had great difficulty in functioning in my daily tasks.

Next came *anger*, which lasted a few weeks. I was so angry with Mary that I could not stand to be around her, and when I was, I would give her the silent treatment. I was also angry with God for not intervening to prevent Mary from betraying me. I let Him have it one day during my prayer time. Home alone and face down on the floor praying, I suddenly exploded with anger and began yelling at God at the top of my voice: "How could You allow this to happen? Why didn't you stop her?"

I am grateful God reveals in Scripture that He can handle outbursts of emotion. In Exodus 5:22, we see Moses' voice his anger toward God saying, "Why, Lord, why have you brought trouble...?" King David also railed at God saying, "Is it not You, God, you who have now rejected us and no longer go out with our armies?" (Psalm 60:10).

While we do not know the tone and volume of Moses' or David's words, it is plausible that theirs was an impassioned, heartfelt cry. In all cases, God knows exactly how we feel and wants us to be honest in sharing our feelings with Him.

Lastly, I plunged into *depression and detachment.* For nearly 20 years, I was often emotionally distant from Mary, the kids, family, and friends. I would attend social gatherings but barely engage. Instead, I chose to feel sorry for myself.

Work became my only source of satisfaction—at the neglect of everything else in my life. During that time, I looked for every opportunity to travel on business to get away from my wife and kids. It may sound strange, but when I was at work, I would not think about Mary's betrayal. It was a welcome distraction.

THE JOURNEY TO FORGIVENESS

The Oxford Dictionary defines *forgiveness* as *to stop feeling angry or resentful (toward someone) for an offense, flaw, or mistake; to pardon, excuse, exonerate, or absolve someone.* Dr. Charles Stanley describes forgiveness as "the act of setting someone free from an obligation to you that is the result of a wrong done against you."

A few months after her confession, I told Mary that I forgave her. I essentially checked the box because I knew I was supposed to do that as a believer in Christ. My mouth said it, but there was no true forgiveness in my heart. My attitude and actions toward my wife did not change.

It's well said that "Unforgiveness is like drinking poison and expecting the other person to die." For many years, my life illustrated this quote. I was bitter, miserable, depressed, insecure, ashamed, and void of emotional connection to my wife and children. I became critical and demanded perfection from them. Trying to hide my emotions from others caused me to wear an invisible mask each day.

Worse yet, shame kept me from telling anyone what I was going through. This prevented me from receiving confidential counsel or prayer by mature believers who could have helped. I later had to repent from my nasty attitude and actions towards others. I had to work hard to heal those hurts and reestablish the relationships that I damaged.

Hebrews 12:14-15 exhorts us to "Make every effort to live in peace with everyone and to be holy; without holiness no one will see the Lord. See to it that no one falls short of the grace of God and that no bitter root grows up to cause trouble and defile many." Every effort would be needed to pull up those roots of bitterness in my soul.

GOD'S MANDATE TO FORGIVE

Then Peter came to Jesus and asked, "Lord, how many times shall I forgive my brother or sister who sins against me? Up to seven times?" Jesus answered, "I tell you, not seven times, but seventy-seven times." – Matthew 18:21-22

Forgiveness is the message of the cross. Jesus came to extend God's forgiveness to us, and in turn, God requires us to forgive others. He requires forgiveness because He loves us and knows what is best for us. Forgiveness is what sets us free. It removes the poison of bitterness from our soul, and the lie that we are the one who can rightly judge a person.

We must remember that we are not the judge of anyone— only God is. When we forgive the person who hurt us, we acknowledge that God will rightly mete out justice and mercy. The Bible assures us "Will not the Judge of all the earth do right?" (Genesis 18:25b).

Once we forgive, sometimes the offender will be brought to a place of repentance and in some cases seek to reconcile with those he or she has hurt. In our case, Mary had already turned away from her sin before she confessed it to me.

You may have offenders who have not yet repented of their wrongdoing toward you. That is a difficult place to be. Jesus understands. He modeled for us what we should do when we are in that situation. As He suffered on the cross, Jesus prayed, "Father forgive them, for they do not know what they are doing."[3]

5 PRINCIPLES OF FORGIVENESS

1. Forgiveness is not based on the other person's actions or apology, but on your choice to forgive as God requires. Forgiveness can involve reconciliation, but sometimes that is not possible. You can choose to forgive, while not restoring the relationship.
2. Forgiveness does not downplay or erase the memory of what happened; however, the pain will gradually lose its power over you.
3. Forgiveness is more of a process than an event. Seemingly unrelated issues, even from childhood, may emerge which will need to be addressed. God wants to heal the whole of you.
4. Forgiveness is a conversation between you and God and effective when you verbalize the offender's name and their specific offense(s) against you.
5. Forgiveness includes any need to forgive yourself.

FORGIVING YOURSELF

Many times, we can forgive others but have difficulty forgiving ourselves. As you learned, I had great difficulty in forgiving my wife, but I also struggled with forgiving myself for my sin of pornography. I repented and experienced God and Mary's forgiveness, as well as healing from the addiction.

However, even then, I found it difficult to forgive myself. The memory of my sinful behavior would creep up from time to time. Whenever the vile images I had seen would flash in my mind, I would often descend into self-condemnation and shame. Years later, I was finally able to share these feelings with a Christian counselor who wisely said, "If God has forgiven you, who are you to not forgive yourself? Are your standards higher than God's?" His words made me realize that grace was to be extended not just to others, but to me as well.

Forgiveness does not mean forgetting. While the memories of the offense(s) will remain, in time they will no longer have power over your life. The devil will not be able to push those buttons any more to afflict you.

LOOKING MORE LIKE JESUS

I am happy to report that forgiving Mary led to a full reconciliation and restoration of our marriage! God reintroduced me to my wonderful bride and gave me a renewed appreciation of the gift that she is. I regained the desire to spend time with her and our closeness has not only grown but blossomed. We both feel more in love than ever! Mary and I are now completely aligned in purpose, and totally trust and respect one another. By God's grace, we are coming up on our 42nd wedding anniversary.

With my new attitude, I sought restoration also in my relationship with my now adult children. I had to humble myself, repent, and ask each of them to forgive me for all the years that I was withdrawn and emotionally distant. I am thankful that the Lord was gracious to restore those relationships as well.

I pray that my story helps you realize that God is willing and able to heal your broken relationships. However, to do that, you must drop the emotional rocks you are holding onto and forgive the person or persons who hurt you. Keep in mind that forgiveness is only attainable when you do it God's way. Forgiveness may sometimes be more complex than you think due to repeated "injuries" that may compound the most prevalent of all past offenses. I encourage you to seek the help of a skilled Christian therapist. I can also recommend books like

Off the Hook: How Forgiving You Frees Me by Tibbitts and Goldberg[4] or *The Gift of Forgiveness* by Charles Stanley.[5]

Soon after our relationship was healed, I was reminded of a prayer I had prayed daily for several years in my early walk with Jesus. It was, *"God, make me a man after your own heart."* It was then that I heard His affirming words resonate deep within me, *"Son, I did."*

CHAPTER 5 REFLECTION

1. In a spirit of extending the same forgiveness you received from God to others, ask the Holy Spirit to show you if you harbor any bitterness or unforgiveness in your heart toward someone.

2. If the answer is yes, write down the name(s) of those who have hurt you and the specific offense. Each must be dealt with individually.

3. Go before your Heavenly Father and for each person on your list, verbally declare their name and specific injury for which you are forgiving them. It is common for emotions to emerge.

You may find it difficult to get the words out of your mouth, but when you do, you will be actively setting yourself free from the trauma of the past and the poison of bitterness that has adversely affected your life. As Luke 6:37 states, "Do not judge, and you will not be judged. Do not condemn, and you will not be condemned. Forgive, and you will be forgiven."

ACHIEVING AN INNER RADIANCE

For God, who said, "Let light shine out of the darkness," made His light shine in our hearts to give us the light of the knowledge of God's glory displayed in the face of Christ. But we have this treasure in jars of clay to show that this all-surpassing power is from God and not from us. — 2 Corinthians 4:6-7

We have taken an honest look in the mirror and submitted ourselves to the purifying work of the Holy Spirit by removing all idols and the darkness that does not belong in the holy places of our hearts and minds. Now it's time to fill ourselves with more of what does belong! This is a necessary step of preparation for every member of the Bride-Church. There is an inherent beauty we are destined to display for the glory of our heavenly Bridegroom. This internal radiance comes not from ourselves, but from Christ's Spirit with whom we are called to be filled.[1] The more we have of Him, the more brilliantly we will shine!

Remembering that God uses what is familiar in the physical realm to help His people understand greater spiritual truths, we return to look at the Most Holy Place where God's glorious Spirit hovered over the Ark of the Covenant. It is here where we discover that the contents tucked inside the Ark unlock the secret to receiving great measures of God's Spirit and inherent light.

Each item stored within shows us what should reside in the sacred places of our hearts and minds. As we peek inside, these iconic symbols are not to be viewed through the *old covenant of the law* as given through Moses, but rather through the lens of the *new covenant of grace* that Jesus secured for us. The Bible explains, "But in fact the ministry Jesus has received is as superior to theirs as the covenant of which He is mediator is superior to the old one, since the new covenant is established on better promises" (Hebrews 8:6).

There were three items placed inside the Ark: a jar of *manna*, the stone tablets of the covenant or *Ten Commandments*, and *Aaron's budded and blossomed staff*.[2] Each provides powerful imagery to the treasures every believer's heart should hold.

A HEART FULL OF JESUS

The first item preserved inside the Ark was a jar of *manna*. Manna was the bread from Heaven—honey-like wafers that God provided for the Israelites to eat while they wandered in the wilderness for 40 years.[3] The manna served as life-giving sustenance and pointed toward the true Bread and Giver of life, Jesus.

Although manna could not prevent physical death, the spiritual bread Christ provides through His broken body and spilled blood on the cross promises every partaker the gift of eternal life. The sacrament of Holy Communion reinforces our remembrance of this truth. The presence of the manna in the Ark is a strong declaration of the preeminence of Christ. He is manifested there by His Holy Spirit who indwells us upon our confession of faith. The Gospel of John confirms this truth:

> *So they asked him, "What sign then will you give that we may see and believe? What will you do? Our ancestors ate the manna in the wilderness; as it is written: 'He gave them bread from Heaven to eat.'" Jesus said to them "Very truly I tell you, it is not Moses who has given you the bread from Heaven, but it is My Father who gives you the true bread from Heaven. For the bread of God is the bread that comes down from Heaven and gives life to the world.'*
>
> *"Sir," they said, "always give us this bread."*
>
> *Then Jesus declared, "I am the Bread of Life... I am the living bread that came down from Heaven. Whoever eats this bread will live forever. This bread is my flesh, which I will give for the life of the world"* –John 6:30-35, 51

A HEART FULL OF TRUTH AND LOVE

The second item placed inside the Ark was the stone tablets of the covenant known as the *Ten Commandments* that God gave Moses on Mt. Sinai. Immense blessings are promised for those who are obedient to God's Word, and negative consequences are promised to those who are not.[4] The spiritual significance of the tablets is multi-faceted.

Just like the manna, the Ten Commandments are symbolic of Jesus. John 17:17 tells us simply that "God's Word is truth." As the true, inerrant, written Word, the Bible is fully embodied in Jesus. He is the fulfillment of every commandment and exists as the *Word incarnate*. The Gospel of John declares,

> *In the beginning was the Word, and the Word was with God, and the Word was God. He was with God in the beginning... In Him was life, and that life was the light of all mankind... The Word became flesh and made His dwelling among us. We have seen His glory, the glory of*

the One and Only Son, who came from the Father, full of grace and truth." –John 1:1-2, 4, 14

The presence of the tablets in the Ark illustrates the importance of having not only Jesus' abiding Spirit within us, but also His Word. Placing your faith and trust in the Son of God welcomes Him into your heart—but reading and getting to know Him through the pages of Scripture is what brings us into a deeper relationship. From start to finish, the Bible reveals who Jesus is, what He has done, what He is doing, and what He will do. Scripture also reveals His love, mercy, grace, power, faithfulness, righteousness, suffering, promises, resurrection, and the eternal hope found in Him.

Jesus knew the importance His teachings would have in the life of His people and admonishes us to keep His commands within us. "Keep My commands and you will live; guard My teachings as the apple of your eye. Bind them on your fingers; write them on the tablet of your heart" (Proverbs 7:2-3).

Spending time in the Bible is one of the most valuable activities you can do. Unlike common books, the Bible is living and active and will speak directly into your life wherever you are and in whatever circumstance you may be going through.[5] It is the guidebook for life, as well as a cleanser for the soul through which Jesus washes every member of His Bride-Church. As shared in Ephesians 5:25-27 "...Christ loved the church and gave Himself up for her to make her holy, cleansing her by the washing with water through the Word, and to present her to Himself as a radiant church, without stain or wrinkle or any other blemish, but holy and blameless."

The tablets being placed within the Ark also point to the new covenant, *the law of grace and love*. "When questioned about which is the greatest law by the religious leaders, Jesus began, 'Love the Lord your God with all your heart... This is the first and greatest commandment. And the second is like it: Love your neighbor as yourself'""" (Matthew 22:37-39). Romans 13:10 summarized further: "Therefore love is the fulfillment of the law." These Scriptures emphasize that in keeping God's commands, our external obedience must be motivated by an underlying attitude of love.

A HEART FULL OF OBEDIENCE

The third item kept inside the Ark was Aaron's miraculously transformed staff. Moses and Aaron were appointed by God to serve alongside one another. Moses was leader over the Israelites, while Aaron served as their high priest.

When rebellion arose, the Lord settled the matter by instructing Moses to take one staff from each head of the 12 tribes and to inscribe Aaron's name upon his staff. Each of the 12 staffs were then placed inside the Tent of Meeting where God convened to make clear His choice of high priest. Aaron's staff not only budded and sprouted but also produced fruit. This was an undeniable sign that Moses and Aaron were indeed God's chosen instruments to lead the nation. The budded staff also put an end to the people's grumbling.[6]

The presence of Aaron's staff within the Ark serves as a reminder to guard against any rebellion that may rise in our hearts. Members of the Bride-Church should be steadfast to accept and obey whatever God says.[7] A life of obedience is a blessed life. A life of obedience produces fruit. This beautiful picture is painted for us in Psalm 1:1-3:

> *Blessed is the one who does not walk in step with the wicked or stand in the way that sinners take or sit in the seat of mockers, but whose delight is in the law of the LORD, and who meditates on His law day and night. That person is like a tree planted by streams of water, which yields its fruit in season and whose leaf does not wither—whatever he does prospers.*

BEAUTY FOR ASHES

> *The Spirit of the Sovereign LORD is on me, because the LORD has anointed me to proclaim good news to the poor. He has sent me to bind up the brokenhearted, to proclaim freedom for the captives and release from darkness for the prisoners, to proclaim the year of the LORD's favor and the day of vengeance of our God, to comfort all who mourn, and provide for those who grieve in Zion—to bestow on them a crown of beauty instead of ashes, the oil of joy instead of mourning, and a garment of praise instead of a spirit of despair.* – Isaiah 61:1-3

One counter-intuitive way God fashions His Bride-Church to reflect more of His light is through the working of trials and suffering in our lives. Every person in this world suffers. No one is exempt. Suffering is not a respecter of race, color, creed, social status, or position. Suffering can lead to depression, hardened hearts, even despair without the help and hope of the resurrected Savior. Suffering is a shared human experience and can come about in one of two ways: either *despite* Jesus or *with* Jesus. Our Savior tells us, "In this world you will have trouble. But take heart! I have overcome the world" (John 16:33b).

Suffering can present itself *despite* Jesus as a result of our sinful nature and its consequences. We all have experienced painful repercussions from personal failings. We also suffer when someone else's sin affects us—through no fault of our own. The world is filled with victims who have been physically, mentally, emotionally, sexually, or spiritually abused. Many are wounded by neglect, betrayal, denial, exploitation, or rejection. People also suffer due to the fallen state of our physical world. We experience the tragedies caused by natural disasters, disease, and death. We need to look no further than our own lives and the evening news to see the widespread suffering in our communities and around the world.

Suffering can also happen *with* Jesus, as believers coura-geously take a stand with Him and are persecuted for their faith. Nations, tribes, and communities continue to victimize Christians who openly follow Jesus. As part of today's world-wide persecuted church, many believers are tortured, impris-oned, and even martyred. At the start of this decade, *Christianity Today* reported that modern persecution of believers worldwide hit an all-time high with "260 million Christians suffering high to severe levels of persecution."[8]

While suffering with Jesus is real, the Apostle Paul offers hope to those enduring it by reminding us, "The Spirit Himself testifies with our spirit that we are children of God, and if chil-dren, heirs also, heirs of God and fellow heirs with Christ, if indeed we suffer with Him so that we may be glorified with Him" (Romans 8:16-17).

THE PURPOSE OF SUFFERING

Becoming glorified with Jesus is our destiny. However, Scrip-ture reminds us that it's the testing of our faith through trials that will develop our perseverance to make us mature and complete in Christ.[9] Regardless of the source, suffering changes us. Life happens, and the devil will do all he can to use traumatic events to hurt us more deeply. Consequently, Jesus' Bride-Church may not only find herself in need of physical healing, but spiritual healing as well. We have an enemy who "comes only to steal and kill and destroy" (John 10:10).

Nonetheless, God knows each one of us perfectly and uses every trial to strengthen our faith in the places where it is weak so we can learn how to be overcomers. With this in mind, every difficult circumstance should be viewed as a training ground for the Church to learn how to humbly co-reign with her King Jesus. Suffering is the necessary pre-requisite to rulership because rulership in the Kingdom of God requires character, and character is only developed through suffering. Be encouraged to know that "If we endure, we shall also reign with Him" (2 Timothy 2:12).

THE REFINER'S FIREPOT

As a result of both of our moral failures, Joseph and I suffered for years, fighting to save our marriage. Thankfully, God was with us, and we ultimately experienced victory through His faithfulness and grace. Through it we learned that life is a journey full of joys and sorrows, all of which are used to refine us. We wish we could tell you that there was a one-and-done lesson, but alas, that is not the case. We encourage you to keep your heart open to more of what the Lord wants to teach you in your life and specific circumstances.

Some life lessons are harder than others. Another season of intensive learning came to our family in 2004. This is the year Joseph and I have come to refer to as our *year of hell.* Have you ever had one of those? Perhaps you have, but we recognize that some have not. If you have not, you may be unable to relate to what I am about to share. However, you may know of a loved one or friend who is going through something similar, and the spiritual lessons learned here may offer some perspective and help.

As God would have it, at that time I was teaching a women's Bible study going through the Gospel of Luke. One day as I was preparing, I came to Luke 22:31 where Jesus told Peter that he was about to be *sifted* by the devil. At that moment, God spoke those same words to my heart in preparation for what was about to transpire. "Mary, Mary, Satan has asked to sift you as wheat. But I have prayed for you, Mary, that your faith may not fail. And when you have turned back, strengthen your sisters and brothers."[10] What happened shortly afterward was a spiritual attack for which we were sorely ill-equipped.

In our family of five, we suddenly began experiencing bizarre happenings with our health, finances, relationships, and well-being. Intense stress, depression and anxiety soon followed. There was also a dark spiritual presence in our home that could be physically seen, heard, and felt. I am not trying to get weird, but it *did* get weird. We even had mushrooms growing out of our carpet in the corner of our dining room. They came from a leaky pipe in the wall, but the mushrooms represented a fitting picture of the vile fungus that was attempting to overtake us. Things rose to ridiculous levels, but we weren't laughing.

The Apostle Peter speaks of believers being tested by fire saying:

> *Dear friends, do not be surprised by the fiery ordeal that has come on you to test you, as though something strange were happening to you. But rejoice inasmuch as you participate in the sufferings of Christ, so that you may be overjoyed when His glory is revealed.* −1 Peter 4:12-13

Peter's use of the word "strange" was the right description for what was happening to us. We found ourselves deep in the *firepot*—undergoing testing that went beyond anything we had experienced previously.

THE MASTER METALSMITH

In the process of purifying precious metals of silver and gold, the raw materials are heated over a fire to the point of lique-faction. This causes the impurities, or *dross*, to rise to the top so the metalsmith can then skim them off. This process is repeated until the reflection of the metalsmith can be seen upon the molten surface. Only then are precious metals ready for use.

God uses a similar process with us. He allows the testing of our faith to heat up to just the right temperature in order to cause the impurities in our hearts to surface so they can be skillfully extracted. Proverbs 25:4 explains, "Remove the dross from the silver, and a silversmith can produce a vessel." As a result of the time spent in the refiner's firepot, you will come forth purified as silver and gold, through which others can see a mirror reflection of God—the *Master Metalsmith*.

As our family struggled through that year, one particular day stands out. Joseph and I were in the kitchen when we received word of more bad news. I grabbed my husband's shirt with both hands, buried my head into his chest, and began to physically shake and cry out in anguish. Neither of us could understand what was going on. We were a Christian family actively serving the Lord in our community and ministry. Our children and household were dedicated to Him, and yet God was allowing so much evil to overtake us. To make matters worse, He was seemingly absent, even silent in response to our fervent prayers. We found ourselves desperate for answers and relief. It was at that moment that I needed God's perspective.

It is easy to praise the Lord when things are going well, but what about when they are not? As I was tormented with my thoughts, it was then that I heard a voice in my head almost audibly tell me to "curse God." Matthew 12:34 warns, "For the mouth speaks what the heart is full of." I am not proud to say that in my weakness and vulnerability, I came *very close* to doing that. I stepped to the edge of the cliff as my soul violently battled within me.

I had a decision to make that would become a defining moment in my life. How genuine was my faith? Did I really believe? Did I really trust? Did God really love us, and if so, where was He?

LESSONS FROM JOB

Most are familiar with the biblical story of Job. A righteous man who is described as "blameless and upright, a man who fears God and shuns evil" (Job 1:8). Job was wealthy, and he would regularly offer sacrifices for his ten children just in case they had somehow sinned and "cursed God in their hearts" (Job 1:5).

One day the angels, including Satan, presented themselves before God. There the Lord had a conversation with the devil about His faithful servant Job. Questioning the authenticity of Job's faith, Satan falsely accused Job of fearing God only because he was blessed with a hedge of protection around him and everything he possessed. The devil said, "But stretch out Your hand and strike everything he has, and he will surely curse You to Your face" (Job 1:11).

So, the Lord granted the devil permission to afflict Job as a test of his faith. Satan got right to his dirty work and in one day struck down Job's livestock, herdsmen, servants, home and *all ten* of his children.[11] It is recorded that "At this, Job got up and tore his robe... fell to the ground in worship and said: 'Naked I came from my mother's womb, and naked I will depart. The LORD gave and the LORD has taken away; may the name of the Lord be praised'" (Job 1:20-21).

In a second test of his faith, Job was afflicted with painful sores all over his body. His wife, who should have been a source of comfort and love, instead said "Are you still maintaining your integrity? Curse God and die!" (Job 2:9). Please, get this perspective. THAT is the devil's end game—to get each one of God's people to believe his lies and become so miserable, broken, and defeated that we curse God—and die!

Despite unfathomable suffering, Job's trust in his Maker remained steadfast as he made the declaration, "But He knows the way that I take; when He has tested me, I will come forth as gold" (Job 23:10). And he did shine forth as gold! At the end of the ordeal, God was pleased and not only restored Job, but blessed him back two-fold. Everything Job had before he was afflicted was doubled. He even fathered ten *more* children.

Joseph and I in no way compare our trials that year to the magnitude of Job's, but I remember having this moment of clarity that Satan was orchestrating a coordinated attack on our family. His goal was to apply so much pressure that we would turn from our faith and curse God. It was upon this realization that my entire perspective changed. By the grace of God, I was able to reach into the core belief of my heart and make a choice to audibly praise Him, and I did it in a way that the old devil and his cohorts could hear it!

I didn't connect it at the time, but the Bible offers this encouragement:

> *In all this you greatly rejoice, though now for a little while you may have had to suffer grief in all kinds of trials. These have come so that the proven genuineness of your faith—of greater worth than gold, which perishes even though refined by fire—may result in praise, glory and honor when Jesus Christ is revealed.* −1 Peter 1:6-7

It was not long after my pronouncement of praise to God that the enemy retreated, and our home was peacefully restored. Miraculous deliverance is released when we learn to praise our God amid the storms of life. Through that challenging season, our family learned to ask not the question of *WHY* a trial has come, but instead to ask the question of *WHAT*. What does God want us to learn through this? As a result, we are now better equipped for the trials of life. But even more, we remain forever grateful and eternally changed.

English poet Robert Browning penned these profound and wise words that resonate as true:

I walked a mile with Pleasure;
She chatted all the way;
But left me none the wiser
For all she had to say.
I walked a mile with Sorrow;
And ne'er a word said she;
But, oh! The things I learned from her,
When Sorrow walked with me.

CHAPTER 6 REFLECTION

1. Take a moment to reflect upon the contents within the *ark of your heart*. How may God be leading you to focus your efforts on having more of:
A Heart Full of Jesus?
A Heart Full of Truth and Love?
A Heart of Obedience?

2. Romans 5:3-5 declares: "...suffering produces perseverance; perseverance, character; and character, hope. And hope does not put us to shame." Think of one challenge you have suffered in life that God used to develop your character. How were you changed? What was the result spiritually?

OBTAINING AN OUTER GLOW

CLEANSING OUR OUTER COURTS

One of the many things our family learned about spiritual warfare during 2004 was the importance of not only purifying the inner temple courts of our hearts, minds, and bodies, but also the outer courts of our *external spaces*. As I mentioned in chapter 6, there was an actual presence of evil in our home. As children of God and members of Christ's Bride-Church, how was that even possible? This question propelled us to seek answers.

The Apostle John offers this great truth: "You, dear children, are from God and have overcome them, because the One who is in you is greater than the one who is in the world" (1 John 4:4). Because of this fact, *we can be assured that the devil can never possess a true believer's heart, as the Holy Spirit is the sole resident.*

However, Satan can and will try to oppress, harass, or afflict believers. The devil is a bully who uses intimidation tactics to deceive people into believing that he is to be feared. However, as a defeated foe, he and his demons tremble before the living God, who dwells within us. James gives us this insight: "You believe that there is one God. Good! Even the demons believe that—and shudder" (James 2:19).

Until the devil is permanently removed from the earth, he continues to war against the faithful. Be careful of his tactics. Even the best of us can fall. Consider Peter whom Satan used as his mouthpiece. Jesus rebuked him by saying, "Get behind Me, Satan! You are a stumbling block to me; you do not have in mind the concerns of God, but merely human concerns" (Matthew 16:23).

Not only will the enemy try to put words in our mouth that do not belong, but he can also try to enter our households through unholy objects that do not belong. Such things must be removed with great diligence. Even Jesus swept clean the outer courts of the Temple in Jerusalem twice. John 2:15 recounted one such scene when Jesus "made a whip out of cords, and drove all from the temple courts, both sheep and cattle; he scattered the coins of the money changers and overturned their tables."

Jesus zealously demonstrated the importance of keeping our homes, property, and personal spaces unpolluted from that which defile. He gives His followers the confidence and authority to take action in purifying our spaces. Jesus said, "I have given you authority to trample on snakes and scorpions and to overcome all the power of the enemy; nothing will harm you" (Luke 10:19).

One of the devil's names is Beelzebub which means "lord of the flies." Just as garbage attracts flies, objects of darkness can attract demons. There are many Scriptures that clearly state that there are objects that God strictly forbids us to have.

THE FIRST TWO of the Ten Commandments state:

> *"I am the LORD your God, who brought you out of Egypt, out of the land of slavery. You shall have no other gods before Me. You shall not make for yourself an image in the form of anything in Heaven above or on the earth beneath or in the waters below. You shall not bow down to them or worship them; for I the LORD your God, am a jealous God."*
> –Exodus 20:1-5a

God is ferociously jealous for His people. In fact, *Jealous* is one of His names.[1] In Hebrew, the word *jealous* is defined as *used of God as not bearing any rival; the severe avenger of departure from Himself.*[2] Our Eternal Husband will not put up with sharing us. We are His alone. To flirt with any other god through owning graven images is an affront to Him.

Not only that, but out of His omniscient love, He desires to protect us from that which could bring harm. Deuteronomy tells us why, "For you are a people holy to the LORD your God. The LORD your God has chosen you out of all the peoples on the face of the earth to be His people, His treasured possession" (Deuteronomy 7:6). God knows the destruction that can come from idolatry and possessing graven images, so He wants us to stay far away from them.

THE SIN OF RACHEL

The danger graven images can bring into our lives is best illustrated in Genesis chapter 31. After serving his Uncle Laban for 20 years, Jacob (later named Israel) left Laban's house and set out with his wives Leah and Rachel, and their numerous children and livestock. Jacob was abundantly blessed.

However before departing, Rachel secretly stole her father's household gods. Hiding them inside her camel's saddle, she sat on them. When Laban realized his idols were missing, he chased down Jacob and angrily accused him of stealing his gods. Not knowing one of his wives was the thief, Jacob adamantly denied it and spoke a curse, "If you find anyone who has your gods, he shall not live."[3] Laban then searched through Jacob's possessions and failed to find anything. To Rachel's discredit, both men had been fooled.

Sometime later, trouble started coming to Jacob's house. Jacob wrestled with God and ended up with a limp. His daughter Dinah is raped. In a vigilante rage, his sons Simeon and Levi seek revenge through a bloody killing spree—making Jacob and his family a stench to the neighboring communities. Jacob's lament is recorded. "We are few in number, and if they join forces against me and attack me, I and my household will be destroyed" (Genesis 34:30b). Oh Rachel! What did you do? Divine intervention was needed, and spiritual housecleaning was the instruction for relief.

In Genesis 35:1-5 God said to Jacob:

"Go up to Bethel and settle there, and build an altar…" So Jacob said to his household and to all who were with him, "Get rid of the foreign gods you have with you, and purify yourselves and change your clothes…" So they gave Jacob all the foreign gods they had and the rings in their ears, and Jacob buried them under the oak at Shechem. Then they set out, and the terror of God fell on the towns all around them so that no one pursued them.

Later, in seeming fulfillment of Jacob's curse, Rachel died an early death while birthing their second child. But let's not miss this—it was *after* Jacob and his family got rid of their forbidden idols, discarding them in the first recorded landfill, that God blessed him once again and his enemies fled! *Getting rid of idols is not a guarantee that you'll avoid difficulties in life but getting rid of idols is something God commands us to do for our own good.*

THE SIN OF THE ISRAELITES

The sin of idolatry is one that is often repeated in Scripture. As Moses descended Mt. Sinai carrying the Ten Commandments, he came into the Israelite camp and saw the people had cast an image of a golden calf. Sacrifices were being offered to it, while the people indulged in debauchery. In righteous anger God threatened to destroy them all, however Moses interceded, and the LORD relented with a less severe judgment.[4]

Mindful that the Israelites were prone to this form of sin, before they could enter the Promised Land, God directed them to destroy every pagan nation. No treaties were to be made, nor were they allowed to intermarry, as this would turn their hearts once again to the idols of foreign gods. His instructions were:

> *"This is what you are to do to them: Break down their altars, smash their sacred stones, cut down their Asherah poles and burn their idols in the fire. For you are a people holy to the LORD your God ... Do not bring a detestable thing into your house or you, like it, will be set apart for destruction. Regard it as vile and utterly detest it, for it is set apart for destruction."* –Deuteronomy 7:5-6, 26

THE SIN OF ACHAN

God is serious about His people keeping their lives spiritually pure. We see the consequences of rebellion play out once again with the sin of Achan. After conquering Jericho, Achan took some of the booty and hid it in the ground under his tent, disobeying God's strict instructions not to touch any of the spoils of war. As a result, the Lord's anger burned against Israel.[5]

Because of Achan's disobedience, disaster came to the Israelite community as they were soon defeated by a comparatively small army. Supposing it to be an easy victory, Joshua did not understand why they had lost the battle. It is recorded that Joshua sought the Lord until evening.

Recorded is God's robust response to Jacob:

> *"Stand up! What are you doing down on your face? Israel has sinned… they have taken some of the devoted things… lied… and put them with their own possessions… that is why the Israelites cannot stand against their enemies… I will not be with you anymore unless you destroy whatever among you is devoted to destruction."* –Joshua 7:10-13

Lots were drawn and Achan's sin was discovered. God then directed that Achan, and his family be killed as punishment. God was sending the strongest of warnings that we are to watch what we bring into our tents! This is not about God denying us something that would bless us. This is not about God being the decorator police. This is about a jealous God wanting to protect his children and Jesus' Bride-Church from that which can bring devastation to our families, community, and even our nation.

Sometimes God allowed the Israelites to keep the booty from a battle victory. Sometimes He did not. As a protective Father, He knows exactly what would bless His children and what would curse. God's instructions are never arbitrary but are to be trusted and obeyed. In all things we must "Trust in the LORD with all your heart and lean not on your own understanding; in all your ways submit to Him, and He will make your paths straight" (Proverbs 3:5-6).

The commands God gave in the Old Testament regarding keeping our lives spiritually clean were put into action in the New Testament by the early Church. In the book of Acts, the Apostle Paul ministered in the city of Ephesus where cultic practices were common. When people saw the power of God at work through Paul's preaching of Jesus, many Ephesians came to faith and destroyed their objects of darkness. The Bible records:

Many of those who believed now came and openly confessed what they had done. A number who had practiced sorcery brought their scrolls together and burned them publicly. When they calculated the value of the scrolls, the total came to 50,000 drachmas. In this way the Word of the LORD spread widely and grew in power. —Acts 19:18-20

This scene highlights the fact that some items do need to be burned to be utterly destroyed.

Here is the connection we need to make. Since early human history, people have used inanimate objects to commune with demons. Demons use graven images to receive worship from people by attaching themselves to the object. In and of themselves idols are powerless things—just wood, clay, metal, or stone. But those who possess these items (knowingly or unknowingly) leave themselves vulnerable to dark powers and influence.

Some unclean objects can sit in your homes quietly for years, even being handed down generation to generation. They do not seem to cause any problems. However, unclean items provide a portal of entry to harass, oppress, or wreak havoc against you and your family should the enemy decide to use them. In his letter to the Corinthians, Paul wrote, "Do I mean then that food sacrificed to an idol is anything, or that an idol is anything? No, but the sacrifices of pagans are offered to demons, not to God, and I do not want you to be participants with demons" (1 Corinthians 10:19-20).

How do we liberate our lives of unclean objects so that we can achieve a brilliant shine in our Outer Courts? Through a pre-emptive attack.

5 STEPS TO CLEANSING YOUR OUTER COURTS

Just as God did with the Israelites, if you seek Him, He will equip and lead you through the process of removing things in your life that do not belong. In John 14, Jesus explains where our help comes from: "'But the Advocate, the Holy Spirit, whom the Father will send in My name, will teach you all things ... Peace I leave with you ... Do not let your hearts be troubled and do not be afraid'" (John 14:26-27).

Here are 5 STEPS to help you cleanse the Outer Courts of your life:

1. Ask the Holy Spirit to lead you.
2. Do a thorough search through your house and find items that need to be removed. Look for objects related to past sin or ungodly/toxic relationships, representations of darkness or the devil (serpent, dragon, etc.), false deities or cultic religions, Freemasonry, pornography, witchcraft, fortune-telling, astrology, superstition, Mardi-Gras type masks (these symbolize a hypocrite/liar), Ouija boards, death, New Age, or mystical objects, etc. The enemy may try to discourage or distract you from parting with such items. Stay vigilant and on task.
3. Destroy and discard what you find. Don't pass a problem on to someone else.
4. Ask forgiveness as you renounce each item in the name of the Lord Jesus Christ.
5. Dedicate all you have to God—giving Him thanks for setting you free!

RESPONSIBLE CLEANSING

But if I drive out demons by the finger of God, then the kingdom of God has come upon you. − Luke 11:20

Before I began to spiritually cleanse our house, I sought my husband's blessing. This is important because the spirit world recognizes the authorities God has set in place with Christ as the Head of His Church, the husband as head of the wife and family, and parents over their children.[6]

It is helpful if you can go through this process together, but this is not always possible. As you are one flesh with your spouse, you have the right to get rid of things that belong to both of you, but wisdom dictates that you respectfully seek agreement to keep peace in the relationship. You are only allowed to discard what belongs to you, or things that you have been given permission to remove. If you are separated from your spouse, you can remove their items by returning them or asking permission to discard.

Regarding items belonging to young children, the responsibility to remove what does not belong lies with you. However, it is a little different with older children or teens as they own their own possessions to some degree. Because you own the house in which they live, you have the final say about what gets brought in, hung on their walls, what type of music and games they can play, and what activities are done while they are in your house. It is important to respect their privacy and property. When something needs to be removed you should take time to explain the reason in an age-appropriate way, without causing any fear, confusion, or superstition. If you get resistance, consider replacing the item(s) with something better or compensate them for it. These considerations will help to maintain a peaceful relationship.

PURIFYING THE HOME

In a large house there are articles not only of gold and silver, but also of wood and clay; some are for special purposes and some for common use. Those who cleanse themselves from the latter will be instruments for special purposes, made holy, useful to the Master and prepared to do any good work. Flee the evil desires of youth and pursue righteousness, faith, love and peace, along with those who call on the Lord out of a pure heart. – 2 Timothy 2:20-22

As I began spiritually cleansing our home, I prayed the Holy Spirit would lead me. Then I started searching through closets, drawers, and cabinets. I combed through our entire house. As a Christ-centered home, we did not have any blatantly bad items, but as God began to open my eyes, I was shocked at what I found.

There were some books about religious cults in my library, video games and music that had dark scenes and lyrics, earrings from an old boyfriend—which was dishonoring to my husband, a gold horn or *cornicello*—which is an amulet of superstition to protect from evil, a beer stein painted with hooded druids, some New Age artistic glass pieces, seemingly innocent movies that glorified witchcraft, a theatrical mask, and more.

Some would think that I went overboard in what I eliminated, but I chose to err on the side of caution rather than error. If it was iffy, I threw it away for peace of mind. It did not matter the value of the item. It did not matter the sentiment. Some things were given by parents, grandparents, loved ones and friends. When I hesitated to discard some of these items, this Scripture came to my mind: Jesus said, "'If anyone comes to me and does not hate father and mother, wife and children, brothers and sisters—yes, even their own life—such a person cannot be My disciple'" (Luke 14:25-26). I chose to honor God, even if that meant getting rid of something that a beloved family member had given to us.

The Greek word to *hate* is defined as *to love less*.[7] Jesus obviously does not advocate that we despise our family members, but we are called to love God more. It took several years to go through this process of cleansing our house, but in time God revealed what needed to go.

THE LESSON OF DAGON

There is a story in 1 Samuel 5:1-6 where the Philistines captured the Ark of God from the Israelites, carried it into the temple of their god Dagon and set it right beside the statue of Dagon. When the Philistines rose the next morning, there was Dagon, fallen on his face on the ground before the Ark of the Lord. Propping him up, they put him back in his place. But the following morning, there was Dagon once again—fallen on his face! This time, his head and hands were broken off. The Scripture records that as a result, the Lord's hand was heavy upon the people—bringing devastation and affliction upon them.

As stated earlier, you need to ask the Holy Spirit to show you what does not belong in your home. Some things may appear harmless. I had a porcelain figurine of a woman which my grandmother had given me. I kept it as a little treasure atop our bedroom dresser. It had fallen over a few times. One time her head broke off, another time her arm and hand. Each time I glued her back together.

One day I decided to do a little redecorating, and one of our daughters told me to get rid of it. I picked up the figurine and gently rested it on its side on the sofa in our room. After a while, I sat down next to the statue. Suddenly, my eyes were opened! There on the bottom of the statue written with a gold pen was the signature of the artist and in large font, his numbering of the piece "666."

It was here where I learned *the lesson of Dagon.* The porcelain statue had been devoted to the devil, and for years God was trying to get me to throw the cursed thing away by having it repeatedly break. Unwittingly, I kept gluing it together and propping it back up! Pay attention when things break, there may be a good reason.

DECLARING OWNERSHIP

If you own your home, you have legal ownership. If you lease your home, you have temporary legal ownership like a hotel room or any other rented space. It is important that when you gain possession of property, you make a declaration in the name of the Lord Jesus Christ that the property belongs to you, and everything unclean brought in by any prior owners must leave. Invite the Holy Spirit to fill your dwelling and property with His presence and peace. Declare Psalm 91 over it. Praise God for His love, goodness, and protection!

WORTH THE WORK

Spiritually cleansing your outer courts can take some time and effort, but it is worth the work. It will change the entire atmosphere of your home. A few years after we cleared things out, we had some missionary friends stay with us while they were in town visiting. The next morning before they left the wife said to me, "Mary, your home is so filled with God's peace. There's an extra measure here that I can feel!" Without telling her any of our stories, I just smiled and said, "Thank you."

God was compassionate and gracious to help us turn our

once chaotic home into a sparkling sanctuary of safety and comfort for our family and guests. The Lord desires for every member of His Bride-Church to "live in peaceful dwelling places, in secure homes, in undisturbed places of rest" (Isaiah 32:18).

CHAPTER 7 REFLECTION

1. On a scale of 1 to 10 (1 being the worst, 10 being the best), assess the *spiritual peace level* in your home.

2. Commit to taking the time to begin cleansing your outer courts (home, workspaces, vehicles, property, etc.). This is different than what we traditionally see as "spring cleaning" or a decluttering effort. The 5 Steps listed in the above chapter will help walk you through the process.

3. As you work through each room in your home, invite the Holy Spirit to guide you. It may be helpful to journal about your experience and reflect on the lessons you learned through the process.

BECOMING A BRILLIANT REFLECTION

THE PARABLE OF THE TEN VIRGINS

The *Parable of the Ten Virgins* recounted in the book of Matthew is perhaps the single most important instruction Jesus gives for us to know how we can be *confidently* ready for the Splendid Day when He returns to rapture His Bride.

Alarmingly, Jesus prophetically warns that only half of those watching and waiting for His return will be prepared. That means that 50 percent of those who claim to know Christ will miss the Rapture! This sobering statistic emphasizes Jesus' statement that on the day when He comes "one will be taken and the other left" (Matthew 24:40).

God's heart is that *no one* would be left behind. To this end, Jesus teaches through this paramount story what we need to know in order to prepare:

"At that time the kingdom of Heaven will be like ten virgins who took their lamps and went out to meet the bridegroom. Five of them were foolish and five were wise. The foolish ones took their lamps but did not take any oil with them. The wise, however, took oil in jars along with

their lamps. The bridegroom was a long time in coming, and they all became drowsy and fell asleep.

At midnight the cry rang out: 'Here's the bridegroom! Come out to meet him!' Then all the virgins woke up and trimmed their lamps. The foolish ones said to the wise, 'Give us some of your oil; our lamps are going out.' 'No,' they replied, 'there may not be enough for both us and you. Instead, go to those who sell oil and buy some for yourselves.' But while they were on their way to buy the oil, the bridegroom arrived. The virgins who were ready went in with him to the wedding banquet. And the door was shut. Later the others also came, 'Lord, Lord.' They said, 'open the door for us!' But he replied, 'Truly I tell you, I don't know you.' Therefore, keep watch, because you do not know the day or the hour." –Matthew 25:1-13

The word *virgin*[1] in Greek refers to a marriageable female or male who has been kept sexually chaste. The Apostle Paul expands on the definition of *virgin* as one who *is concerned about the Lord's affairs: Her aim is to be devoted to the Lord in both body and spirit* (1 Corinthians 7:34). There exists an inherent connection between one's body and spirit.

Five of the ten virgins were described as *foolish*, while the other five were described as *wise*. Interestingly, all ten virgins recognized that it was time for the bridegroom to arrive, and they expectantly ventured out together to meet him. The bridegroom took longer to come than they had anticipated, and while waiting they all fell asleep.

In biblical times, it was common for the bridegroom to arrive around midnight with a shout and the blowing of a ram's horn or *shofar* to alert the village. Accompanied by an entourage, the groom would joyfully make his way to the house of his bride to sweep her away to their new home at his father's house, where the wedding celebration would occur. It was an event not to be missed.

Lamps, typically made of jars of clay, were used in

wedding processions to provide illumination, and add to the festivity of the event. The wise virgins were ready with their lamps and carried along with them the oil needed to fuel them. Contrarily, the foolish virgins also had lamps, but did not take any oil. Although the fools waited alongside the wise, their lack of preparation would prove costly.

To help us properly comprehend this important message, we must first understand the meaning of the elements and the order of how Jesus tells the story. In the Bible, a *lamp* is often used to symbolize the Word of God.[2] However, it is also used as a metaphor to describe the spiritual vessel of our hearts.

Second Corinthians 4:6-7 explains that God has made His light shine in our hearts, and *we hold this treasure in jars of clay*. Likewise, *oil* is figuratively used to symbolize the Holy Spirit.[3] With that in mind, many make the mistake of interpreting the parable by *prematurely* applying the ascribed spiritual meaning to these everyday objects. Contrary to popular practice, Jesus did not. Sometimes in storytelling a lamp is just a lamp, a light is just a light, and oil is just oil. Initially, this is how these elements should be viewed.

In fact, Jesus provided specific clues to help us avoid applying the spiritual symbolism *too soon*. The mentioned oil could not have been the oil of the Holy Spirit yet, as evidenced in the wise virgins counseling the foolish ones to go buy some. This would have contradicted New Testament Scriptures. If the oil was intended to represent the Holy Spirit, the wise virgins would never have suggested such a blasphemous thing. They would have known that the Holy Spirit is a *special oil* that cannot be bought. In Acts 8, Simon the Sorcerer offered the apostles money to buy the Holy Spirit and was harshly rebuked for such a wicked thought![4]

The other clue Jesus gave to help us correctly interpret the parable was that the foolish virgins' lamps were going out when the bridegroom arrived. If the oil represented the Holy Spirit, and their scant amount was almost gone, it would dangerously imply that the Spirit could run out, dry up, be lost, or taken away. This would be contrary to what God has promised. Instead, the Holy Spirit seals us and will always remain with every person who has put their trust in Christ.[5] *Therefore, the first portion of the parable must be interpreted at face value.*

Because the wise virgins were prepared, when the cry rang out that the bridegroom had arrived, they were able to immediately trim their lamps and depart. Not so for the fools. They began to panic because their lamps were running on fumes and about to extinguish. *What caused their crisis? A lack of personal responsibility.*

Jesus paints this stark picture to highlight that it is up to each individual to have what is needed. Obviously, there was ample time to secure the needed oil as it was an anticipated event. The virgins knew the bridegroom was coming and was running later than they expected. Jesus was right to describe five of them as *moros,*[6] which means *dull, stupid, godless.*

When the foolish virgins realized their lamps were going out, they proceeded to ASK the wise if they would share their oil. The wise virgins refused and told them to go and buy some for themselves. This would be nearly impossible to do as it was midnight, and the shops were closed. Still, they departed to SEEK the oil they needed. Unfortunately, it was too late.

The wise virgins were not selfish in their refusal, they knew they had just enough oil for their own lamps, and it was time to depart. Without delay, they were able to follow the bridegroom into the wedding feast, after which time *the door was shut.*

It is at this juncture that Jesus moves the parable from a story of a common wedding celebration to the future Messianic banquet. *It is also here where biblical symbolism should now be applied.* Latecomers are hardly excluded from wedding receptions, but when the foolish virgins arrived, they were denied entrance. Though they would KNOCK and ASK that the door be opened, to their horror, the bridegroom turned them away saying, "I tell you the truth, I don't know you." The parable concludes, "Therefore keep watch, because you do not know the day or hour." The Greek word *watch*[7] means *take heed, be vigilant, give strict attention lest through remissness some destructive calamity suddenly overtakes you.*

The application is clear. *Spiritual preparation cannot be borrowed or bought, rather it is up to each individual to ASK, SEEK, and KNOCK to receive the oil of the Holy Spirit by receiving the Lord Jesus Christ into the vessel of your heart before it is too late!* Securing this figurative oil ahead of the Bridegroom rapturing away His Bride-Church is everything. The foolish virgins were as strangers to the bridegroom. They assumed that he would know who they were, but he did not. Some of you may wonder, "Why not?" After all, the five did hold a trace amount of oil that managed a glimmer of light.

The book of Romans explains that God supplies every person with a measure of light so that they are without excuse. First *externally*, seeing God's existence through His glorious creation.[8] Second *internally*, knowing God exists by our consciences that bear witness to His law written upon our hearts, so that every person can discern between what is right and wrong.[9] These two powerful forms of evidence serve as *fire-starters.* Sparks which have the potential to ignite the heart aflame as one sees there is a holy God with a holy standard of which we all fall short.[10]

It's not enough to recognize that there is a God. Many do. It's not enough to know the difference between good and evil and purpose to live a noble life. Many do that as well. It's also dangerously deceptive to believe that just because you were raised in a Christian home or attend church, that you will be saved. No, the only way to Heaven is through repentance of your sin and a heartfelt confession of faith in Jesus. Romans 10:9-10 explains, "If you declare with your mouth, 'Jesus is

Lord,' and believe in your heart that God raised Him from the dead, you will be saved. For it is with your heart that you believe and are justified, and it is with your mouth that you profess your faith and are saved."

Your salvation and ticket for the Heaven-bound flight of the Rapture all depends on having the Holy Spirit of Jesus in your heart and nothing else. It is a gift from God that must be received. It cannot be earned. "For it is by grace you have been saved, through faith—and this not from yourselves, it is the gift of God—not by works, so that no one can boast" (Ephesians 2:8-9).

Asking, seeking, and knocking to receive the Holy Spirit by faith in the heavenly Bridegroom is not complicated, nor difficult. God makes it easy, but *you have to do it*. And the incredible thing is that once you put your faith in Jesus to secure your salvation and receive the initial sealing and filling of the Spirit —a transformation will begin.[11]

How much of His presence and transformational power do you want in your life? It really is up to you. Feel like you are running on fumes? Ask and seek for more of the Holy Spirit, and more you will receive! God is not stingy when it comes to pouring into His people, for He "gives the Spirit without limit."[12] In fact, the Apostle Paul tells us to pursue being filled to the brim.[13] In Luke 11:9-13, Jesus tells us exactly how:

"So I say to you: ASK and it will be given to you; SEEK and you will find; KNOCK and the door will be opened to you. For everyone who ASKS receives; the one who SEEKS finds; and to the one who KNOCKS, the door will be opened. Which of you fathers, if your son asks for fish, will give him a snake instead? Or if he asks for an egg, will give him a scorpion? If you, then, though you are evil, know how to give good gifts to your children, how much more will your Father in Heaven give the Holy Spirit to those who ask him!"

The fire of my faith was lit by confessing to God that I was a sinner and praying to receive Jesus into my heart. It was then that I became sealed and indwelt with the Holy Spirit for salvation. Sometime after, I decided to join a Bible study. This made a tremendous difference, as I needed to learn Jesus' teachings so that I could apply them to my life. Because my greatest sin came *after* I accepted Jesus as my Savior, it would be correct to say that at that time I was more spiritually aligned with one of the five compromised lampstand churches Jesus addressed in the first part of Revelation. (See chapter 4 or Appendix A.)

As I began growing in the understanding of God's Word, one day an older, godly family member explained to me that unless I seek after the Holy Spirit, I would be limited in my understanding, growth, and relationship with Jesus. It was then that I began an intentional search to learn more about the third person of the Trinity.

Because I knew very little about the Holy Spirit, I began asking the Lord to give me what I needed and then earnestly sought out Bible verses, books, devotions, sermons, and more mature believers in our church to help me. It came about that one evening after I put the kids to bed, I felt compelled to spend some time praising and thanking God. Suddenly, the fill spout of my heart's lamp opened wider, and God's Spirit poured in.[14] It was transformational! In receiving more of the Spirit that night, it was like the wattage of Christ's light within me intensified, and my spiritual understanding and gifting increased in ways I never could have imagined.

But even more than that, my love and devotion to Jesus also grew in a way that I would say crossed me over from being in the *compromised church* category to the *faithful church* category. Please understand that it wasn't a physical change of churches, but rather a sanctifying change that happened in my heart!

The love for my heavenly Bridegroom became first and foremost, and I no longer desired the things of the world, but only to live in a way that would please Him.[15] It was soon after that I gained the courage to put my faith in action by obediently confessing my sin to Joseph. I began to do as Colossians 1:10 admonishes: "live a life worthy of the Lord and please Him in every way: bearing fruit in every good work, growing in the knowledge of God."

Now, let's get back to the Parable of the Ten Virgins. Perhaps you were raised in a Christian home, or you attend church or classify yourself as a "seeker of truth." However, you have yet to give your heart to Jesus. If this is you, you are lacking the oil of the Holy Spirit and live in danger of missing the Rapture. You have been deceived to think you may be saved already, but Jesus says, "I do not know you." As the five foolish virgins did, you will stand outside knocking and pleading for Him to open the door, but He will not. You may try to reason with Jesus by saying how you ate and drank with Him (perhaps you have participated in the taking of Holy Communion), and how you have even heard His teaching, but Jesus will answer, "I don't know you or where you come from. Away from Me... you evildoer" (Luke 13:25-27).

Thankfully for you, it's not too late! Until the day you die or the Day when Jesus returns, there is still time to secure your salvation. Mark 1:15 announces, "'The time has come ... The kingdom of God is near. Repent and believe the good news.'" There is a suggested prayer of salvation offered in Appendix C at the end of this book.

Repentance is something everyone needs to do. Only God knows your heart. Every unbeliever must humble himself through repentance and accept the Savior to cross over from death to life. Surely the thief on the cross, who was crucified next to Jesus, confessed he was a sinner and professed a true believing faith in Jesus as Savior. The thief had a true deathbed conversion. With no time to do anything else, his faith was sufficient, and he was promised on that day that he would enter paradise with Jesus.[16]

All saved believers, who are in the process of readying themselves for the Day when the beloved Bridegroom comes to rapture them, should also repent of the sins for which the Holy Spirit will bring conviction. Five of the seven churches Jesus addressed in Revelation were implored to repent in preparation for His coming. An active turning away from our sins is something that is motivated by love for our Bridegroom and is achieved by the Spirit of God.

The book of Romans is brimming with the foundational doctrines of our faith. Here we learn about the essential role the Holy Spirit plays in our repentance for both salvation *and* sanctification. Paul writes,

If anyone does not have the Spirit of Christ, he does not belong to Christ... And if the Spirit of Him who raised Jesus from the dead is living in you, He who raised Christ from the dead will also give life to your mortal bodies through His Spirit, who lives in you. –Romans 8:9b, 11

In other words—if you have the Holy Spirit of God within you, whether you die or are still alive on the Splendid Day when the Lord returns to rapture His Church, you will be raised!

FIRSTFRUITS AND THE 144,000

Taken up to Heaven at the Rapture, members of the Bride-Church will be a kind of *firstfruits* to God, with Christ being first and foremost.[17] The Greek word for firstfruits means *to take away the first fruits of the production of the earth which was offered to God; used of persons consecrated to God for all time.*[18] James 1:18 describes the Bride-Church: "He chose to give us birth through the Word of truth, that we might be a kind of firstfruits of all He created." You'll notice language in the coming pages about the harvest of believers. This is where the imagery begins—with the *firstfruits.*

Even as the Bride-Church is harvested and taken from the earth to Heaven, simultaneously there will be another select group of firstfruits. Apart from the Jewish believers who will be raptured and counted as members of the Bride-Church, there will be a select 144,000 Jewish believers marked with a seal on their foreheads to protect them from all harm as they remain on the earth during the time of the Great Tribulation.[19] This *remnant*[20] comprised of physical descendants of Abraham, Isaac, and Jacob will consist of 12,000 taken from each of the 12 ancestral tribes of Israel. In fulfillment of the covenant God made with Abraham, they will be "purchased from among men and offered as firstfruits to God and the Lamb."[21]

Described as virgins, the 144,000 keep themselves pure and will not defile themselves with sexual or other heathen temptations available in the last days under the lawless rule of Antichrist. When the Bride-Church is taken up and no longer present as Christ's witness, this elect remnant of Israel will remain on the earth. They are the Bridegroom's loyal attendants and are described as meek and humble—their voices rising up from the earth in a new song before the throne of God. Even while the inhabitants of the earth suffer during this time, the 144,000 will live righteously in peace and safety—speaking no lies, while patiently waiting for their Messiah's return.

Theologian John Walvoord adds, "In contrast with many others who become martyrs, these people live through the period. But they are not the only ones to survive, as many Gentiles and Jews will turn to Christ in the end time and somehow escape martyrdom and be honored to welcome Christ at His return."[22] Remaining on special assignment, the

144,000 will faithfully serve and follow *Yeshua* (Jesus) wherever He goes once He touches back down on the earth at His Second Coming.[23]

GROWING IN RELATIONSHIP

Looking at the firstfruits of the Bride-Church and the 144,000 remnant, it is clear that these are the ones who are in a deep relationship with their *first love*, Jesus Christ. It is quite the opposite for five of Jesus's seven churches as described in the book of Revelation. Although considered one of His lamp-stands, their lives speak differently, and they are called out for living apart from a healthy relationship with Him. One such church is characterized as lukewarm in their relationship with Christ and in danger of being spit out.[24] He confronts this church with their deception of indifference and calls to those whose hearts may be shuttered so they will once again open their hearts to Him.

The Bridegroom's words to this last church extend to all who have fallen out of intimacy with Him. "Those whom I love I rebuke and discipline. So be earnest and repent. Here I am! I stand at the door and knock. If anyone hears My voice and opens the door, I will come in and *eat* with that person, and they with Me" (Revelation 3:19-20). If you fall within this lukewarm category, now is your opportunity to change!

FELLOWSHIP THROUGH DINING

In the human experience, intimate fellowship can be found around the dining table. When we break bread with another person, something powerfully relational takes place. It can become the impetus that turns an *acquaintance* into a *friend*. In Latin, the word *companion* means *one who eats bread with another.* Jesus set the stage by breaking bread with others throughout

His earthly ministry—both in small settings, as well as with the multitudes.

One day the Bride-Church will physically dine with Jesus at the heavenly Marriage Supper of the Lamb. (This will be further explored in chapter 10.) However, until that day, we can sup with Him now. It's what friends do, and *friend* is what He calls us![25]

There are two *spiritual meals* the Bridegroom invites us to partake in order that we might grow in relationship, friendship, and intimacy with Him. These two meals are the participation of Holy Communion and the feasting on God's Word.

INTIMACY THROUGH COMMUNION

The sacrament of *Holy Communion* or *Eucharist* was instituted by Jesus at the Last Supper when He broke bread with His disciples on the night He was betrayed. Jesus declared in John 6 that He is the *Bread of Life,* and that whoever comes to Him will never go hungry.

The consecrated elements of bread and wine used in Holy Communion are transformational reminders of Christ's sacrifice on the cross, and that through His broken body and shed blood our sins are thoroughly atoned. It is an atonement that provides both spiritual and physical healing. To regularly partake of the elements at His table is a commandment Jesus gave in Luke 22:19 when He said, "This is my body given for you; do this in remembrance of Me."

The sacrament of communion is an intimate act reminding us that corporately we make up *one Body* with Christ. The word *consume* shares the same root as *consummate.* Although our union with Jesus is non-sexual, the act of taking communion carries the idea of joining ourselves to Him as a sign of our shared eternal covenant. This union should not be neglected.

From the marital union of a man and woman we can draw

certain principles of intimacy with Christ. The sexual act in a marriage is of such importance to the ongoing health of the relationship that the Apostle Paul instructs married couples *not to neglect* the coming together so that Satan will not be successful in his temptations.

Many make the mistake of viewing sex as purely a carnal act. This is what the devil wants us to believe, so that lust will have its power over us. But sex is so much more! According to Scripture, sex has a spiritual element where a man and woman not only connect their bodies but spirits as well, fortifying the marital bond.[26]

Paul says that for *special circumstances and a defined time with mutual consent*, we can weaponize our prayers by *fasting from sex*. This is an often-overlooked precept that is an immensely effective tool that can break the power the enemy may have on your marriage, children, or family.[27]

To break the darkness pornography had over our marriage, Joseph and I denied our flesh by fasting from sex one day for every year it had a hold on us.[28] During this time, we committed to focused prayer as a couple and partook in regular communion. Daily, we remembered Jesus's victory over our sin and Satan by uniting ourselves with Him through Holy Communion. At the end of the fast, we came together in spirit, soul, and body. We were finally able to experience true freedom and healing from that which had held us in bondage. By purposing to fully honor God with our bodies[29] through observing the covenant we share with Christ first, we experienced an intimacy with the *Lover of our Souls* we had never known before.

FEASTING ON GOD'S WORD

Intimate fellowship with the heavenly Bridegroom is also gained through digesting the bread of God's Word. As you invest time daily in reading your Bible and becoming a doer of what you learn, you will gain a greater oneness, appreciation, and love for Jesus. Just as close friends or couples over time learn how each one thinks, acts, even what they will speak before they say it, the more time you spend in the Scriptures, the more you will come to know the steadfast love, nature, and voice of Jesus. Feasting on God's Word brings a level of relationship with Jesus that is unsurpassed. Paul expressed these very feelings when he said everything was a loss compared to "the surpassing worth of knowing Christ Jesus my Lord."[30]

Before you begin reading your Bible, ask the Holy Spirit for eyes to see, ears to hear, a heart to perceive, and a mind to understand the wonderful things God desires to speak and show you.[31] You will soon discover words, phrases, sentences, or concepts being highlighted. God's Word will speak directly into your life. It is a remarkable experience! Guidance, counsel, and encouragement are readily available as you turn to the Living Word.[32] Scripture stands the test of time and speaks to people in every generation. The table He sets before us will never run out of nourishing food for the soul.

A continual feast of God's Word is meant to be enjoyed with others who hunger and thirst for righteousness. Jesus modeled this every time He fed the multitudes. You will find great blessing as you give thanks to God for the truths He has revealed to you—and then share this spiritual food with others. Peter was exhorted to feed Christ's sheep, and we are to do the same.[33]

TWO-WAY CONVERSATIONS

The taking of Communion and regular Bible reading is essential. However, if you are not careful, these activities can become ritualistic. As with any healthy relationship, two-way communication is vital. Your heavenly Bridegroom longs to converse with you. Worship and prayer are intrinsic parts of the two-way conversation and are not limited to scheduled times. What is important is that your communication with God is done genuinely in spirit and truth.[34]

We generally consider worship as singing songs and hymns, but the act of worship can encompass so much more. There is a myriad of ways to express what is in your heart. The Greek word for *worship*[35] is defined as *any service*. King David worshipped through dance. Worship is also expressed through good works in the investing of your time, talent, and treasure. The 10 percent tithe of your income to your local church, as well as additional offerings invested in Kingdom work is also a form of worship. Worship should not only occur at Church services but should be a daily outflowing of your love for God. Serving Christ with a glad heart in your home, workplace, or community shines as one of the most beautiful forms of worship.[36]

Prayer is also part of the two-way conversation with the Lord. When we pray, we share the praises, confessions, thanksgiving, and honest concerns of our hearts. God is big enough to handle our grievances, disappointments, hurts, joys, hopes, and dreams. At the outset, you may find yourself doing more talking than listening. But over time, prayers can shift toward listening more to what God wants to say to you.

Listening prayer is quite effective and can be experienced by going on a quiet walk, meditating with praise music, or taking in an evening sunset. Jesus loves spending time with you. Psalm 17:6 encourages us in our prayer life by assuring that when we call on God, He will answer us. He will turn His ear toward us and hear our prayers. Your prayers matter and are powerful and effective![37]

OUR SABBATH REST

As the Bride-Church, we should be mindful that even as we do our part to be sanctified, read our Bibles, worship, and pray— our Bridegroom is *not* a taskmaster. Quite the contrary! Believers are *liberated* into His Sabbath-rest. Just as God rested from His work on the seventh day of creation, those who trust in Christ enter the same rest He achieved for us.

Salvation can never be earned or kept by our own efforts or performance, but *only* by what the Savior has done in His completed work on the cross. Knowing this, we are now motivated to do everything out of love. There is nothing more we can do or add to what the heavenly Bridegroom accomplished for His Bride-Church. Even so, we are called to keep the Sabbath Day.[38] A rested Bride is a beautiful bride. A rested Bride brings God glory.

NOTICEABLY DIFFERENT

When members of the Bride-Church show up differently from the rest of the world, only then will unbelievers take notice in a way that stirs a desire to have what we have. Those who are searching for the truth will be more open to receive Jesus when they see that our once *disfigured* lives have become remarkably *transfigured.* As we prioritize time to privately fellowship with Jesus, a transformation occurs in ways that others can see.

Time alone with the Lord *physically* changes us. Moses is a perfect example. He met regularly with God and spoke face to face, as one does with a friend.[39] The result of these encounters was that Moses' appearance changed—his face became *radiant* with the glory of God! The glow was so intense that when the Israelites saw it, they gave Moses their full attention to hear what the Lord had to say. In the same way, as we spend time with Jesus, our countenance will change. Though you may not see it yourself, it will be apparent to others. A Christ-centered heart results in a Christ-centered life—one that generates a compelling source of light that attracts others towards it. This is a light that is not meant to be kept to oneself, but a light that is meant to be shared.

CHAPTER 8 REFLECTION

1. ASKING, SEEKING and KNOCKING to be filled with the Holy Spirit are terms that implore an intentional pursuit to be made by you. It is essential to secure the sealing and initial filling of the Holy Spirit by repenting and professing faith in Jesus Christ. This is how you receive the free gift of salvation. If you have yet to do that, there is a suggested prayer in Appendix C at the back of this book.

If you are already a believer in Jesus and desire to receive *more* of God's Spirit, take the first step to ASK through prayer. Secondly, begin a quest to SEEK out to learn more about the Holy Spirit. Your final step will be to KNOCK at the place of discovery, asking the Father to pour more into you.

2. When was the last time you celebrated the Lord's Supper? Make plans to participate with your local church, small group, family, or individually as you are led.

3. What is your favorite time spent with Jesus? (i.e., Bible reading, worship, prayer, serving) Consider trying something you haven't done before to experience Him in a new way.

4. If you don't do so already, make it a regular priority to set aside one day a week for a Sabbath rest.

PART 3: WHAT TO LOOK FORWARD TO

THE ROYAL WEDDING IN HEAVEN

As a young man marries a young woman, so will your Builder marry you;
as a bridegroom rejoices over his bride, so will your God rejoice over you. –
Isaiah 62:5

I n April 2002, our entire family flew to Michigan for our cousin Richard's wedding. He was the youngest and last of 14 cousins to tie the knot. This was big. Twenty-three of us from California—our mother, brother, sisters, spouses, and kids —all headed to the Northeast for the celebration. You have heard of the movie *My Big, Fat Greek Wedding*, well this was going to be a *Big, Fat Italian Wedding*—an event we knew we did not want to miss. There were to be 34 bridesmaids and groomsmen in the wedding party and over 500 guests in attendance!

The ceremony was held in a 100-year-old cathedral in downtown Detroit with colored stained-glass windows and ornately carved woodwork. A full choir sang from the balcony accompanied by an orchestra comprised of violins, flutes, trumpets, and harps. The sanctuary was formally attired with an abundance of long-stemmed white roses and flickering candles.

The groom, accompanied by his groomsmen, were first to position themselves at the front of the church, while the wedding march began to play. As the bridesmaids made their way down the aisle and the flower girls trailed behind—carefully dropping their petals, soon everyone and everything was in place.

A lingering pause… then suddenly the trumpets sounded, and the radiant bride appeared. We all rose to our feet as she began to gracefully make her way toward her bridegroom. We couldn't help but gaze at her beauty. Sandra was her name, and she was stunning—a picture of perfection! I remember thinking that my cousin Richard had done well. But, if the truth be known, as much as we admired the bride, our focus quickly shifted from the one walking down the aisle to the one standing at the front of the altar. He was the one we loved and were related to by blood. The groom was the reason we had journeyed there.

WHEN GOD WENT TO THE ALTAR

Traditionally, the first one to arrive and position himself at the front of the marriage altar is the groom. From this unique vantage point, he can watch his lovely bride make her way toward him as she extends her hand and takes her place beside him. Since God is our heavenly Bridegroom, when will He go to the altar?

The answer is that He already did, and the event is recounted for us in Genesis 12:1-3, with the story of Abraham. While God didn't stand before a cloth-draped table at the center of a sanctuary—He went before an altar just the same.

> *The Lord had said to Abram, "Go from your country, your people and your father's household to the land I will show you. I will make you into a great nation, and I will bless you; I will make your name great, and you will be a blessing. I will bless those who bless you and whoever curses you I will curse; and all peoples on earth will be blessed through you."*

It was here that God extended a *verbal promise* to bless one man—Abram (later renamed Abraham)—with an abundant life and legacy of offspring and prosperity. This promise of lineage and fruitfulness is made even more stunning by the fact that Abram and his wife Sarai (later renamed Sarah) were old, and Sarai was known to be barren. For God to keep His promise, He would need to work a miracle in Abram and Sarai's lives, enabling them to have children. Abram's faith was strong, and He believed God would keep this promise![1]

But to receive this inheritance, there was a condition Abram would need to fulfill. God called him to leave all that was familiar—his country, people, and father's household—in order to make his home in the land of Canaan, the Promised Land.

Sometimes the Lord asks His people to venture to new places. Although the journey would require them to face famine and enemies, Abram along with his wife, Sarai, packed up their belongings and began making their way in an act of total obedience.

One day, after battling pagans and defeating their rulers, God sent a mysterious character to pay Abram a visit. *Melchizedek* served as both the king of Salem (Jerusalem) and priest of God Most High. Filled with righteousness, peace and of no known genealogy, Melchizedek transcended time. A personage not fully understood, there is evidence to indicate that Melchizedek was either the preincarnate Christ or a prefigure of Christ through whom Abram would be blessed.

In their meeting, Melchizedek offered Abram the elements of bread and wine. (Bread and wine are prophetic elements Jesus would share at the Last Supper with His disciples with a promise to partake again one day in heaven with His Church.) In turn—as is customary to a *deity*, Abram presented Melchizedek with a tenth of all he had gained in battle.[2]

This was a remarkable exchange! As covered in chapter 1, the first stage of the ancient Hebrew marriage process is called the *shiddukhin*—entailing the preliminary actions leading up to a legal betrothal. Once the father of the groom would select a suitable wife for his son, he would arrange for the son to go to the potential bride's home to meet with her father in hopes to secure the match.

If Melchizedek was indeed an appearance of the preincarnate Christ, as many theologians believe he was, then His transaction with Abram (the father of the future Bride-Church) would suggest that a betrothal agreement had just taken place.[3] For it was upon this exchange that God took His verbal commitment to bless Abram a step further and expanded His original promise to include protection, rewards, and fruitfulness that would make Abram's descendants as numerous as the stars in the sky.

This pledge to Abram—the father of every believer's faith —was destined to produce not only a physical family, but a spiritual one as well! What was Abram's response? He believed the Lord, and it was credited to him as righteousness.[4]

Abram's faith inaugurated the Abrahamic Covenant, in which the LORD's verbal promises were next turned into a *legally binding obligation.* This obligation was of the highest order.

There is a solemn ceremony that was used and common among the regional nomadic tribes for the pledging of a man and woman in marriage. In this ceremony, animals were cut in half and arranged in a manner as to form a walkable aisle that the two agreeing parties could pass between.[5]

While this may sound gruesome to our 21st century ears, the symbolism of blood spoke of the seriousness of the covenant or promise. If one of the parties was to break the covenant, they too may see death. Once the ritual was performed, the covenant was considered irrevocable, even though the consummation and wedding feast might not take place for years.

To solidify the covenant between Abram and the LORD, Abram was ordered by God to prepare for the ceremony with a heifer, goat, ram, dove and pigeon and to cut the first three animals in half and arrange all of them opposite each other forming a pathway. God then put Abram into a deep sleep. While Abram slept, God alone passed between the pieces. His holy presence manifested in a smoking firepot and blazing torch.[6]

Why did God make His way down the aisle alone? It was to demonstrate that the covenant did not depend on Abram— only God. The covenant was sealed by God alone and based solely on the faithfulness of the Almighty. God made an everlasting promise, one that could not be reversed.

COVENANT VERSUS CONTRACT

There is a difference between a *covenant* and a *contract* between two or more people. A covenant is a pledge with a sealing. In the ancient ritual, the covenant was sealed by blood. In contrast, a contract is a secular version of a covenant where one's signature is their oath.

A covenant is an agreement made in trust, whereas a contract is an agreement made under suspicion. A covenant is an agreement based on giving, whereas a contract is an agreement based on the expectation of receiving. A covenant is a taking on of risk and responsibility, whereas a contract exists to limit one's risk and responsibility.

What must be appreciated is that our God is not a contractual god, but a covenantal God! Upon Him alone lies the risk, responsibility, and obligation to bring what was promised to fruition—regardless of our actions or lack thereof.

The covenant God made with Abram was confirmed again in Genesis 17. By this time, Abram was 99 years old and had fathered a son named Ishmael by Sarai's prompting, through her Egyptian maidservant Hagar.

In a desperate attempt to force God's promise of descendants through Abram's seed, Ishmael's conception created much bigger problems than Abram, Sarai or anyone could have imagined. Generations have suffered the repercussions of this grave disobedience. Ishmael went on to father 12 sons, who would become 12 Arabic nations. And today, the Arab nations continue to live in conflict with the Israel

God wanted Abram and His people to understand that although fulfillment of the covenantal blessings was dependent on Him alone, as recipients they were required to walk rightly before Him. To keep them from straying, Abram and his descendants would need a constant reminder. Consequently, the *covenant of circumcision* was instituted. Circumcision is a cutting away of man's fleshly foreskin, signifying they belong to the Lord.

In addition, Abram's name was changed to Abraham—which in Hebrew is similar to "father of a multitude" of nations, implying a look ahead to his descendants. Likewise, Sarai's name was changed to Sarah—meaning "princess", which was fitting for one who would produce kings.[7]

Their new names signify their new identity and roles as God's chosen patriarch and matriarch—from whom would come many nations.

As Romans 9:6-8 explains:

It is not as though God's Word had failed. For not all who are descended from Israel are Israel. Nor because they are His descendants are they all Abraham's children. On the contrary, "It is through Isaac that your offspring will be reckoned." In other words, it is not the children by physical descent who are God's children, but it is the children of the promise who are regarded as Abraham's offspring.

In keeping with His promise, God miraculously opened Sarah's 90-year-old womb to receive Abraham's seed and conceived Isaac. God's covenant of blessings would now be firmly established—for from Abraham came Isaac, from Isaac came Jacob, and from Jacob (later renamed *Israel*) came the 12 tribal sons who came to form the nation of Israel.

It would be under the leadership of Jacob, Joseph, and Moses, that the nation of Israel would begin to flourish. Through Moses the Law was given, and through Aaron the priesthood was established where the animal sacrificial system was initiated.

Israel's rich history would go on to include the Judges, Kings Saul, David, and Solomon, as well as the building of the Temple in Jerusalem. It would be in the Temple, on this tiny spot of real estate atop the Temple Mount, where the glory of the Living God would come to rest. As a direct result, the nation of Israel would rise to a level of stature, security, wealth, and grandeur that no other nation on the face of the earth had ever enjoyed. Kings and queens journeyed to see this magnificent kingdom and marveled!

Sadly, these blessings would be short lived as King Solomon turned his heart away from God. His fall is recorded in 1 Kings 11, recounting how Solomon intermarried with 700 wives and 300 concubines—all who led him astray to follow other gods. As a result, Solomon did evil in the eyes of the Lord. King

Solomon's sin not only hurt himself, but it infected the entire nation—provoking God's jealousy.

As a Husband to Israel, God provided the very best of the land, resources, care, and protection. Nonetheless, like an adulterous wife, the peoples' hearts turned away from Him. In judgment, God divided the nation. Enemies swept in and conquered Israel—exiling God's people to foreign lands. Jerusalem and her holy Temple were destroyed. However, Israel was never forgotten nor forsaken. A *New Covenant* would now be required to redeem her, as Jeremiah records:

> *"The days are coming ... when I will make a new covenant with the house of Israel and Judah ... It will not be like the covenant I made with their ancestors ... because they broke my covenant, though I was a husband to them ... This is the covenant I will make ... I will put My law in their minds and write it on their hearts. I will be their God, and they will be My people ... For I will forgive their wickedness and will remember their sins no more."* –Jeremiah 31:31-34

This New Covenant was one that only the heavenly Bridegroom could fulfill. Whereas the Old Covenant of keeping the Mosaic Law (Ten Commandments) could never be kept apart from living a sinless life, it did point forward to the New Covenant of grace based on faith in Jesus Christ—the sinless Lamb of God. [8] No more would God require animal sacrifice for the temporary forgiveness of sin, for Christ's sacrifice on the cross was permanent and complete. He mediated the New Covenant, dying as a ransom to set us free from the sins committed under the first covenant.[9]

Additionally, physical circumcision would no longer be required.[10] Instead, God calls all believers to a spiritual circumcision of the heart—marking us as His chosen people and citizens of a heavenly nation. 1 Peter 2:9 affirms, "But you are a chosen people, a royal priesthood, a holy nation, God's special possession." As God's dearly beloved, Jesus is coming back to take us to be with Him forever.

Sitting on an everlasting throne with a reign and kingdom that will never end, Jesus holds many titles including: *King of the Jews, King of Kings, Lord of Lords, the Prince of Peace.*[11] This King, Lord, and Prince is our Eternal Husband. And we long to be forever united to Him in the coming Royal Wedding.

ROYAL WEDDING SONGS

In the book Song of Songs (also called Song of Solomon), the Bible presents a romantic dialogue between a bride and her bridegroom. This poetic book is viewed as a model for marriage, but also serves as an allegory of Christ and His Church.

It is the story of the young Hebrew King Solomon who spots a beautiful maiden who was out tending the vineyards. Embarrassed by the royal entourage, she runs away, but the king could not forget her. Disguised as a humble shepherd, he returns to successfully win her love. Before departing, he promises to make arrangements for their wedding.

As the betrothed waits, she is plagued with doubts that he will ever return. Then one surprising day a royal carriage appears, and she discovers that her shepherd is the king! As the beloved is finally swept away, her heart sings, "Let Him lead me to the banquet hall, and let His banner over me be love" (Song of Songs 2:4).

Psalm 45 poetically sings another royal wedding song. This song is believed to have been written on King Solomon's wedding day, but it is also regarded as a prophecy about Christ and His Bride-Church. Allow your spiritual ears to hear the melody play, as the lyrics penetrate your heart and prepare your mind for the glorious coming of the heavenly Bridegroom at the Rapture.

Shared here are selected portions:

♪♪ *You are the most excellent of men and your lips have been anointed with grace, since God has blessed you forever.*

♪♪ *In your majesty ride forth victoriously in the cause of truth, humility and justice; let your right hand achieve awesome deeds.*

♪♪ *Your throne, O God, will last forever and ever…*

♪♪ *All your robes are fragrant with myrrh and aloes and cassia… the music of the strings makes you glad.*

♪♪ *Daughters of kings are among your honored women; at your right hand is the royal bride…*

♪♪ *Let the king be enthralled by your beauty; honor him, for He is your lord.*

♪♪ *All glorious is the princess within her chamber…*

♪♪ *In embroidered garments she is led to the king; her virgin companions follow her…*

♪♪ *Led in with joy and gladness, they enter the palace of the king.*

THE RAPTURE OF THE BRIDE-CHURCH

The Splendid Day when the Bride-Church will be taken from the earth to meet Jesus in the air is referred to as the *Rapture*. The Greek word is *harpazo*[12] which means *catch up; take by force; catch away; pluck.* This catching up of the bride was an integral part of every ancient Galilean wedding. As the groom came for his bride, she would take a seat on a wooden chair and be lifted off the ground and carried by pole-bearers, as if flying, to her father-in-law's house for the wedding feast.[13] We find the Rapture described in detail here:

> *For the Lord Himself will come down from Heaven, with a loud command, with the voice of the archangel and with the trumpet call of God, and the dead in Christ will rise first. After that, we who are still alive and are left will be caught up together with them in the clouds to meet the Lord in the air. And so we will be with the Lord forever.* —1 Thessalonians 4:16-17

The idea of the bride and bridegroom being caught up together in the air is symbolically incorporated into Jewish weddings to this day. It is represented in a celebratory circle dance called the *horah* where the bride and groom are lifted high into the air on chairs. It is danced to the music of *Hava Nagila*, which translated into English means *Let us rejoice!*

These same words are used in the prophetic biblical announcement of the Wedding Day of the Lamb— "Hallelujah! For our Lord God Almighty reigns. Let us rejoice and be glad and give him glory! For the wedding of the Lamb has come, and His bride has made herself ready" (Revelation 19:6-7).

On the Day of the Rapture, the heavenly Bridegroom, Jesus, will return to earth, the temporary home of the Bride-Church. He will raise the people of His church into the air to meet with Him in the clouds. Together they will ascend to the canopy, or *chuppah*, of Heaven where their covenantal union will be perfected.

Transcending that moment in time and space, Jesus brings His Bride-Church to her eternal home. In this way, our physical, temporary bodies will be made immortal. First Corinthians 15:51-53 shares this exhilarating truth:

> *Listen, I tell you a mystery: We will not all sleep, but we will all be*
> *changed—in a flash, in the twinkling of an eye, at the last trumpet. For*
> *the trumpet will sound, the dead will be raised imperishable, and we will*
> *be changed. For the perishable must clothe itself with the imperishable,*
> *and the mortal with immortality.*

Before the Fall, Adam and Eve were immortal. When the Bride-Church joins the LORD in the air, physical immortality will once again be fully restored. With lightning speed, both the dead and alive in Christ will receive physical, resurrected bodies that will be reunited with our regenerated spirits—perfectly engineered for eternity. The blueprints for our glorified bodies are currently held within our present bodies. Much like a caterpillar transforms into a butterfly, so shall our metamorphosis be.

TIMING OF THE RAPTURE

The Rapture of the Church, when Jesus lifts His Bride-Church off the earth to meet Him in the air to be taken to Heaven with Him, is different from the Second Coming of Jesus when He touches down on the earth to deal with His enemies and deliver God's judgment of wrath.

These are two separate events that happen at two separate times on the prophetic timeline. Although the Second Coming of Jesus will be discussed later in chapter 11 of this book, our focus remains on expecting and preparing for the Splendid Day of the Rapture so that we don't miss it!

Many believers make the mistake of concentrating too much on trying to figure out when the Rapture will happen. Jesus tells us that while we may discern the season of His return, no one knows the day or the hour, except the Father himself. However, because the people of God are called to be ready for Christ's return, it is helpful to understand the various

Biblical views regarding when the Rapture *might* take place.[14] I've provided a brief description of four of the primary Rapture views, as well as what I have come to believe in the paragraphs below.

According to the prophet Daniel, in the Last Days there will be a seven-year Tribulation period, consisting of the most dreadful times ever encountered upon the earth. Mankind's decadence and depravity will reach an all-time high during this time, and God will pour out His judgment and wrath on those who ultimately reject Him.

The *pre-Tribulation* view places the Rapture of the Church *before* the seven-year Tribulation begins. The *mid-Tribulation* view asserts that the Church will be removed sometime at the *halfway point* (or three and a half years) into the seven-year Tribulation. *Pre-wrath Rapture* proponents believe that God will remove His Church sometime *after the halfway point* when Antichrist will be revealed, but before God pours out His wrath.[15] The *post-Tribulation* view places the Rapture at the end of the seven-year Tribulation, asserting that the Church will be on earth during the final judgment period. Pan-Tribulationists jokingly say not to worry about it because "It will all pan out in the end."

Before I share which Rapture view I believe, let me say that I hope that the Pre-Tribulation view is correct! I certainly would not want myself nor my loved ones to be here when the final seven-year Tribulation begins on the earth. I'd rather we all be safely raptured off the earth and in Heaven celebrating with Jesus. That being said—based on my studies of the Last Days, I have taken a more conservative approach and come to align with the Pre-Wrath view.

In Luke 17:24-29 Jesus says the Rapture will happen as fast as lightning and likens the event to the days of Noah and Lot. If we look at what happened to these two righteous men and their families—both had to live through horrifically evil times.

People became so wicked that God decided He needed to cleanse the earth of them. However, the *very day* He would release His wrath of flood on the earth (in the times of Noah) and fire and brimstone (in the times of Lot)—God saw to it that Noah, Lot, and their families would first be brought to safety!

In the same way, the Bride-Church will be kept safe. She will be removed from the earth and taken up to Heaven at the Rapture to be kept from the coming wrath of God. His wrath is described in Revelation as occurring during the second half of the seven-year Tribulation, also known as the Great Tribulation. According to 2 Thessalonians 2:1-4, the day of the Rapture will not come *until* the apostacy (falling away from God) occurs and Antichrist is revealed by setting himself up in God's temple in Jerusalem and proclaiming himself to be God.

This means that the Church will be here for the first portion of the seven-year Tribulation period as God's shining light to the dark world. As she is called to do and has always done, the Church will bear witness to Jesus Christ during this most difficult time—adding to the numbers of those who are being saved by faith up until the time when all believers—dead and alive—will be raptured up.

This firstfruits harvest of believers from the earth are also referred to as the *Tribulation Saints.* In Revelation 7:8-17 they are seen standing before the throne of God and the Lamb (Jesus) in Heaven as a great multitude from every nation, tribe, people, and language. This group of people are specifically identified as those "who have *come out of the Great Tribulation.*"

For those who miss the Rapture and are left behind on the earth to face the horrors of Antichrist, there will still be an opportunity for them to come to faith in Jesus and receive eternal life. These post-Rapture believers will be refined and purified through the intense trials of the Great Tribulation. Because they will not worship the beast (Antichrist) or his image, nor take his mark on their foreheads or hands, this group will face martyrdom. They will be resurrected and gathered as a *second crop* when Jesus returns to the earth in His Second Coming at the end of the seven-year Tribulation.[16] Many in the second harvest of believers will be of Jewish descent.[17]

Although we can hotly debate this topic by pointing to various Scriptures, the timing of *when* Jesus raptures His Church is *non-essential* to our basic Christian doctrine and, as such, diversity of thought should be respected. One thing we can agree on is that no one knows the day or hour. This is why I caution you to never believe anyone who sets specific dates.

Whenever the Rapture occurs on the seven-year timeline, we can take assurance that God's people will not suffer God's wrath. Jesus did that for us.

First Thessalonians 5:9 anchors us in this great assurance: "For God did not appoint us to suffer wrath but to receive salvation through our Lord Jesus Christ."

A WORD ABOUT CHILDREN AND THE RAPTURE

As exciting as the thought of being raptured up to meet Jesus sounds, some of you reading this may be greatly concerned about children, grandchildren, or other young ones who may be left behind. None of us want our cherished loved ones to face the horrifying time of the Great Tribulation alone. Such thoughts may even cause you to want to miss the Rapture, at your own peril, so you can remain on the earth to provide care and protection for them.

If this is you—allow God's Word to give comfort and clarity regarding children and the coming Rapture. First Corinthians 7:14 teaches that if one parent is a believer, accepting Christ as their Savior, then their children are holy. This means that God's spiritual covering would be over your little ones. The covering of protection remains until the child reaches an age of accountability. The age of accountability occurs when a person becomes responsible for their actions before God. The specific age varies from person to person, as each child matures physically, mentally, and emotionally at a different rate. God alone knows that moment when a soul becomes answerable to Him.

However, applying the Jewish culture as a model, the age of accountability is typically 12 to 13 years old: for girls—when she celebrates her *bat mitzvah,* and for boys—when he celebrates his *bar mitzvah.* These religious rituals give recognition before the community that the girl or boy is now considered to have reached the age of accountability.

The Bible records how at 12 years old, Mary and Joseph brought Jesus to the temple in Jerusalem to celebrate the Passover Feast. While his parents were returning home, Jesus intentionally stayed behind. Upon being found days later in the temple courts engaging with the religious teachers, when asked about it, Jesus explained, "Didn't you know I had to be in my Father's house?" (Luke 2:49). Jesus had now come of age and verbally acknowledged that He was accountable to His Heavenly Father first and foremost.

Regarding older or adult children, an unbelieving spouse, parents, or other loved ones, if they have yet received Jesus into their heart as Lord and are at risk of missing the Rapture and being left behind—keep praying! It is God's desire that none should perish. Persistently declare Acts 26:18 over their lives by personalizing this prayer for them: "[O]pen (say person's name here) eyes and turn them from darkness to light, and from the power of Satan to God, so that they may receive forgiveness of sins and a place among those who are sanctified by faith in [Christ Jesus]."

None of us can save anyone, but we can pray for them, share the Gospel as opportunities arise, and most importantly, show them tangible demonstrations of God's love. With family, it is usually what we *do*, more than what we *say* that will win them over to Christ.

BRIDAL GARMENTS

"Let us rejoice and be glad and give Him glory! For the wedding of the Lamb has come, and His bride has made herself ready. Fine linen, bright and clean, was given her to wear." (Fine linen stands for the righteous acts of God's holy people.) – Revelation 19:7-8

Once the Bride-Church is raptured off the earth to meet with her Bridegroom, heavenly apparel will be gifted to every incoming saint. In Revelation 6, we see martyrs wearing white robes in Heaven as they wait under the altar to be avenged.[18] In Revelation 7, the great multitude of people brought out of the Great Tribulation are also described as wearing robes of white.[19] These passages show that the base clothing worn in the heavenly kingdom are the *white garments of salvation* that Jesus provides every believer.

However, for the special occasion of the Wedding of the Lamb, an additional robe—a *linen robe of righteousness*—will be given by Jesus to each member of the Bride-Church as a reward for the good deeds each has done.[20] The prophet Isaiah rejoiced in these garments saying, "I delight greatly in my Lord; my soul rejoices in my God. For He has clothed me with *garments of salvation* and arrayed me in a *robe of righteousness*, as a bridegroom adorns his head like a priest, and as a bride adorns herself with her jewels" (Isaiah 61:10).

The bridal robe of righteousness is a different garment from the first in that it is made of fine linen, bright and clean.

Linen is woven from flax and is the designated material for angels and priests.[21] This lustrous fabric not only shimmers bright and clean but provides a stark contrast to the blood-stained covering of the animal hide God provided to Adam and Eve in the Garden. *Clean* in Greek means *purified by fire.*[22] According to Ephesians 5:25-27, this is the final sanctification of the Bride-Church, when she will be presented to her Bridegroom as a pure virgin without spot, wrinkle, or blemish.

After we are gathered to Jesus, every believer will appear before the gracious Judgment Seat of Christ where their works will be tested by fire and rewarded.[23] *Reward* in Greek means *dues paid for work, wages, rewards God bestows for good deeds.*[24]

First Corinthians 3:12-15 explains that:

> *If anyone builds on the foundation (of Christ) using gold, silver, costly stones, wood, hay or straw, their work will be shown for what it is ... the Day will bring it to light. It will be revealed with fire, and the fire will test the quality of each person's work. If what has been built survives, the builder will receive a reward. If it is burned up, the builder will suffer but yet will be saved—even though only as one escaping through the flames.*

WEDDING GIFTS

In addition to the elegant linen garment each member of the Bride-Church will receive, Jesus will thoughtfully distribute a generous array of other heavenly gifts to those He calls His own:

1. The right to eat from the tree of life (Revelation 2:7)
2. The crown of life and a promise not to experience the second death (Revelation 2:10-11)

3. Hidden manna and a white stone with a new name written on it (Revelation 2:17)
4. Authority over the nations and the morning star (Revelation 2:26-28)
5. A name never to be blotted out of the book of life and acknowledgment before the Father and His angels (Revelation 3:5)
6. The honor to be a pillar in the temple of God. Never again to leave God's presence. The written name of God and the name of the city of God, the new Jerusalem. He will write His new name (Revelation 3:12)
7. The right to sit on His throne (Revelation 3:21)

WEDDING OF THE LAMB

The Wedding of the Lamb will take place at the Bridegroom's home on Mount Zion in the *heavenly Jerusalem* before God—the Judge of all the earth. Scripture suggests that those present to witness this event will be angels, the 24 elders—composed of the 12 apostles and 12 tribal sons of Israel—and the Old Testament prophets, which includes John the Baptist. John has the honored distinction of being called *the friend of the Bridegroom.*[25]

Hebrews 12:22-24 (NASB) describes it this way:

But you have come to Mount Zion and to the city of the living God, the heavenly Jerusalem, and to myriads of angels, to the general assembly and church of the firstborn who are enrolled in Heaven, and to God, the Judge of all, and to the spirits of the righteous made perfect, and to Jesus, the mediator of a new covenant.

Marriage vows are a sacred and intrinsic part of every wedding. They are heartfelt expressions of the depth of love and lifetime commitment each pledge to the relationship. The prophet Hosea and his adulterous wife, Gomer, were introduced back in chapter 2 as an allegory of Christ and His Bride-Church. God instructed Hosea to marry Gomer knowing full well that she would be unfaithful. After giving him children, she left to pursue other lovers. But at God's instruction, Hosea sought her out, brought his wife back, and symbolically remarried her.

In this redemptive story, it is here where we discover the eternal marriage vows God has made to His Bride-Church. Through Hosea, He speaks these tender words, "'I will betroth you to me forever; I will betroth you in righteousness and justice, in love and compassion. I will betroth you in faithfulness, and you will acknowledge the LORD'" *(Hosea 2:19-20).*

"I will betroth you" is repeated three times by the LORD. What is thrice spoken is established and perfected. God wants us to know Him as our Eternal Husband. He binds us to Himself in the most virtuous of ways providing a description of the life that awaits us—*forever in righteousness, justice, love, compassion, and faithfulness.* [26]

CHAPTER 9 REFLECTION

1. Do you feel spiritually ready to be raptured to meet Jesus in the air? Why or why not?

2. Is there something about that Splendid Day that you most look forward to? What is it?

3. As you may have prepared vows for your earthly marriage, are there any wedding vows you would like to make to Jesus? Write down your thoughts.

THE HEAVENLY WEDDING FEAST

Joseph and I were once invited to attend two family weddings within three weeks of each other—both out of town. We wanted to honor our loved ones and personally witness the exchanging of their vows, so we decided to accept both invitations. We are so glad we did! Each celebration was delightful and vastly differed in style and venue.

The first wedding was a dressy affair requesting black-tie attire for which Joseph obliged, while I donned an elegant formal gown. The destination was Tampa, Florida, with the ceremony taking place in a landmark Catholic chapel followed with dinner and dancing at an exclusive Jewish club.

The second wedding was much less formal. The invitation requested *business casual* attire. So Joseph wore a light-weight suit, while I opted for a floral spring dress. The couple exchanged their wedding vows outdoors, beside a creek and under a sprawling willow tree in the gorgeous Indiana country-side. Afterwards, we ate a hearty, home-cooked meal catered by the local Amish.

As we traveled to each event, we packed our suitcases

accordingly. After all, it is important to dress appropriately for a wedding. What you wear matters.

PARABLE OF THE WEDDING FEAST

In the Gospel of Matthew 22:1-14, Jesus shares the *Parable of the Wedding Feast.* As we've focused our attention on the heavenly wedding between Christ and His Bride-Church—we could easily assume Jesus's parable is speaking of the marriage reception that will be thrown in honor of the Bridegroom and His Bride. But not so fast! Yes, one day there will be a literal banquet celebrating our eternal union with Christ. However, the invitation to the wedding feast in Jesus's parable paints a picture of something much greater than festive dining.

Jesus compares the kingdom of Heaven to an earthly king preparing a wedding feast celebrating the marriage of his bridegroom son. Interestingly, the bride is not mentioned. In fact, she appears to be missing from the story! But is she? Initial invitations were distributed even before the story begins, so the invitees were not caught by surprise. They had been preselected and were expected to attend. Because the feast was in honor of the king's son, the invitation was more of a royal decree. The king sends his servants to tell those who had been invited that it was time for the wedding feast to begin. Astonishingly, the announcement was ignored, and the invitees refused to come.

It was common in biblical times for guests to receive a preliminary invitation to a wedding. Approximately one year later, as the betrothal period concluded, a formal announcement would inform everyone that the time for celebrating had come. The father of the groom determined the day and hour of the party. Until then, invitees were expected to anticipate the event and be prepared. Wedding garments were usually provided by the host ahead of time, and it was the guest's responsibility to ensure they were kept clean and ready for wearing at a moment's notice. Today, a *Save the Date* card is frequently sent as a preliminary invite. In this way guests have ample notice to reserve the day on their calendar so that when the formal invitation is received, they can RSVP accordingly and arrive at the appointed time.

As his royal decree is ignored, the king exhibits forbearance by ordering three announcements to be made. Sending additional servants to gather the guests, he provides enticement with a menu of tasty meat—similar to how wedding invitations provide a glimpse of the meal by asking for your entrée selection. Since this was a royal feast, we can imagine the king preparing unlimited portions of every sweet and savory delight to be indulged in by the guests. Anyone in their right mind would consider it a privilege to sit at such an extravagant table!

As the parable continues, an unimaginable scene unfolds. Some choose to ignore the whole affair and instead attend to daily duties. Others mistreat and kill the palace messengers! In response, the king orders his army to destroy the undeserving subjects and their city. Told over 2,000 years ago, this parable has proved to be prophetic and has been partially fulfilled today.

INVITED GUESTS

As God's chosen people, the Israelites were at the top of the guest list. Included were family members and direct descendants of Abraham, Isaac, and Jacob. The Jewish nation was formed by God and blessed above all others, to be a blessing to the world. They were entrusted as God's witnesses to rightly represent Him as the One true God, to deliver the written Word of truth through the Law and the prophets, and to proclaim the coming of the promised *Messiah*. It is only fitting that these honored guests would be the first ones to receive an invitation to the royal Wedding Feast prepared in Heaven for those who love and believe in Jesus.

Unfortunately, in hardness of heart, the Jewish nation widely rejected God's invitation through His servants, the prophets. They ignored and killed many, including John the Baptist, who as the herald of the Messiah boldly proclaimed that the Bridegroom had indeed arrived in the person of Jesus Christ.

Their actions were inexcusable as the Old Testament contains more than 300 prophecies regarding Messiah's first coming. In fact, the pharisees and scribes had received a *Save the Date* card! It was delivered by the prophet Daniel some 500 years earlier in one of the most precise prophecies in all the Bible. By way of a mathematical calculation based on recognizable historical events, Daniel foretold the exact day the Messiah would arrive, and He did! [1] The day is known as *Palm Sunday*—when Jesus rode on a donkey into Jerusalem. Even though the people applauded Him that day, He foretold that they would soon reject Him.

In Luke 19:42-44, Jesus wept over the city of Jerusalem and said,

> *"If you had known on this day, even you, the conditions for peace! But now they have been hidden from your eyes. For the days will come upon you when your enemies... will level you to the ground ... because you did not recognize the time of your visitation."*

Within that same week, Jesus was crucified at the demand of the Jewish religious leaders and at the hand of a Gentile ruler, Pontius Pilate. In fulfillment of Jesus's Word, the nation of Israel fell in 70 A.D. under General Titus of the Roman Empire, who later became emperor. The city of Jerusalem was razed, its people were scattered around the world, and the holy temple was destroyed. To this day, no physical Jewish temple exists—although efforts to rebuild the temple are advancing.

Gratefully, not every person of Jewish descent rejected the invitation to acknowledge and celebrate the heavenly Bridegroom. Certainly, Christ's first disciples were Jewish. These He counted as His *guests*. When asked why His disciples were not fasting, Jesus answered, "'How can the guests of the bridegroom fast while He is with them? They cannot, so long as they have Him with them. But the time will come when the bridegroom will be taken from them, and on that day they will fast'" (Mark 2:19-20).

Nevertheless, due to Israel's national rejection, the invitation to attend the King's Wedding Feast was next sent to the Gentile nations. Over the centuries, countless numbers of men and women have come into the Kingdom of God by responding to His invitation and putting their faith in Christ in a continued fulfillment of the parable to this day. Does this mean that God is done with Israel? Never! He clearly has a special heart and love for her.

In Romans 11:11, 25-27, the Apostle Paul explains:

Did they (Israel) stumble so as to fall beyond recovery? Not at all! Rather, because of their transgression, salvation has come to the Gentiles to make Israel envious ... I do not want you to be ignorant of this mystery, brothers and sisters, so that you may not be conceited: Israel has experienced a hardening in part until the full number of the Gentiles has come in, and in this way all Israel (both a spiritual and physical remnant) will be saved. As it is written: "The deliverer will come from Zion; He will turn godlessness away from Jacob. And this is my covenant with them when I take away their sins."[2]

Because the initial invited guests of the Jewish nation refused to come and God the Father desires his *Wedding Hall* be filled, the invitation has been extended to the Gentiles and anyone who desires to respond. And so it is that the Gospel will make its way onto the highways and byways until people from every nation, tribe, language, and people group are represented, as described in Revelation 7:9. Those from *every nation, tribe, people and language* include those from the physical 12 tribes of Israel. Yes, they too will be present. Even today there is a growing number of Jewish believers who have responded to the King's invitation. Though they were the *first* to receive the invitation, they are also coming in as *last*.[3]

THE KING'S WEDDING HALL

Two questions you may be thinking: Just where is the place of the King's Wedding Hall? And where is the missing Bride? You may find the answers to these questions a marvelous surprise!

The *wedding hall* referenced in Jesus's parable can be somewhat misleading as the English word conjures up images of rented banquet facilities or country club dining rooms. Even if we think of such a space existing somewhere in the heavens, we can still miss the deeper meaning without turning to the original language. The word *wedding hall* in Greek translates to mean *a chamber with a bridal bed; a room where marriage ceremonies are held*.[4] Additionally, the same term *wedding hall* is used for the word *bridegroom*[5] that Jesus used in referring to Himself. How can the wedding hall and the Bridegroom be one and the same?

The cloth canopy suspended by four poles beneath which Jewish marriage traditions have been held for centuries is called a *chuppah*. In biblical times, the chuppah was not a place for public viewing of the ceremonial union of the bride and groom, instead it was a private room or *tent* in which the marriage was consummated. King David equated the tented bridal bed to the bridegroom when he wrote in the Psalms, "In

MARY SOLER

the heavens God has pitched a tent (chuppah) for the sun. It is like a bridegroom coming out of his chamber, like a champion rejoicing to run his course" (Psalm 19:4b-5).

This idea is also presented in the story of the Moabite woman, Ruth, who was married to a man from Bethlehem. Sometime after he died, and she was widowed and left desolate, she sought the benevolence of a kinsman-redeemer from within her husband's tribe. Humbling herself at Boaz's feet, Ruth requested that he "spread the corner of his garment" over her. As Boaz gladly consented, his symbolic act provided tender imagery that he would now be Ruth's covering—her provider, protector, home, and *bridegroom*.[6]

Under the heavenly chuppah of the Bridegroom Himself, Jesus will spread *the corner of His garment* over those who stand before Him. Yes! All who have responded to the wedding invitation—an invitation to accept Jesus as their Savior and Lord —are more than just guests. Corporately pictured together and dressed in white robes, they comprise His beloved Bride-Church. There in His presence, believers in Christ will tabernacle (or dwell) with Him and be forever provided for and protected in the home of our Eternal Husband. This magnificent scene is portrayed in Revelation 7:13-15, and reflects the importance of wearing the proper attire to the heavenly wedding festivities:

Then one of the elders asked me, "These in white robes—who are they, and where did they come from?" I answered, "Sir, you know." And he said, "These are they who have come out of the great Tribulation; they have washed their robes and made them white in the blood of the Lamb. Therefore, they are before the throne of God and serve him day and night in his temple, and He who sits on the throne will shelter them with His presence."

REFERRING BACK to the Parable of the Wedding Banquet, the guests who accepted the invitation received their wedding clothes just as they arrived, for they had come in off the streets. However, one person managed to slip in improperly dressed, and the king took notice. When he asked the wedding crasher how he got in, the man had no acceptable defense. The king then ordered that the intruder be tied up and thrown out where there will be weeping and gnashing of teeth. The message is clear. Regardless of whether the world labels you as a "good or bad" person, what matters is that you humbly accept God's invitation of salvation through Christ by taking off your sinful street clothes and changing into the white robes of righteousness, which the heavenly Bridegroom provides.

THE CONSUMMATION

According to ancient practices, once a bride and groom were wed and before making their first public appearance as husband and wife, they would be secluded away together for seven days to become intimately acquainted with one another by consummating the marriage. Such a *bridal week* was practiced when Leah was given to Jacob as his wife.[7] Also important to note is that the law in Deuteronomy 24:5 requires a newly married man to spend the first year at home with his wife to bring her happiness, before he could go off to war or other duties. Similar practices of honeymooning continue today as couples enjoy time alone together following the wedding ceremony.

The word *consummate* means "to bring to a state of completion; fulfill." The consummation of every earthly marriage covenant is completed with the first marital intercourse— where a man and woman physically unite to become one flesh. The sacred act of a bride and groom experiencing oneness in matrimony is representative of the Day when the Bride-

Church will not only be spiritually joined to Jesus, as we currently are, but abiding physically with Him as well.

Our eternal union with the heavenly Bridegroom will be surpassingly loving and intimate, but non-sexual, as we are already one flesh with Him —members of His body.[8] The Bible is clear that in Heaven people will neither marry nor will be given in marriage, but we will be like the angels in Heaven.[9] Still, when we meet Jesus face to face, a fullness of knowing Him will occur. First Corinthians 13:12 explains, "For now we see only a reflection as in a mirror; then we shall see face to face. Now I *know* in part; then I shall *know* fully, even as I am fully *known*."

In the above verse, the first occurrence of the word *know*[10] in Greek is defined as *to learn to know; to come to know.* Whereas the second and third occurrence of the word *know*[11] means *to become thoroughly acquainted with; to know accurately; to know well; to understand.* One use of the word describes a coming to know someone versus a complete knowing of them. There exists a longing deep within every member of the Bride-Church to know Jesus as best we can this side of Heaven.[12] Every joy we experience here on earth merely hints of greater heavenly delights to come, where natural joy will be supplanted by the supernatural.

As discussed earlier in chapter 8, the partaking of Holy Communion is an intimate act—carrying the idea of joining ourselves to Jesus as a sign of our shared eternal covenant. Once the Bride-Church partakes of the Wedding Supper of the Lamb with the Bridegroom, a divine consummation will occur where we will experience completed oneness with Him. Where He will fill us with joy in His presence, bestowing eternal pleasures at His right hand.[13]

THE WEDDING SUPPER OF THE LAMB

Then the angel said to me, "Write this: Blessed are those who are invited to the wedding supper of the Lamb!" – Revelation 19:9

Indeed, the Parable of the Wedding Feast Jesus told is more about salvation than it is about dinner and dancing. However, one of the pleasures to be enjoyed in Heaven will be the breaking of physical bread together. The Bible supports this idea of angelic and post-resurrection dining. A few examples include biblical references to the angels who visited Abraham and enjoyed a meal of veal, bread, milk, and curds;[14] the bread of angels or *manna* God gave the Israelites to eat while they wandered in the wilderness;[15] and Jesus's post-resurrection snack of broiled fish.[16]

So, too, we will have the joy of communing with our Bride-groom at a specially prepared meal at the Wedding Supper of the Lamb. A table in the *Upper Room of Heaven* will be set as He has promised, and the Father has arranged. Just as He eagerly desired to share the Last Supper with His disciples, He is eagerly waiting to share a new *First Supper* together with His Bride-Church in the Father's Kingdom. Jesus prophesied the future occasion in Matthew 26:29 when in the Upper Room celebrating the Passover with His disciples, He said: "'I tell you, I will not drink from this fruit of the vine from now on until that day when I drink it new with you in my Father's kingdom.'"

A FEAST FIT FOR A KING

There is an often missed but eventful scene in 1 Samuel 9:17-24, 10:1 where God selects Saul to be the first human king over the nation Israel. It describes how Saul is invited to the feasting hall at the high place by the high-priest Samuel and is later anointed to serve as leader over the nation. Saul was divinely selected to co-rule under God Almighty, just as the Bride-Church will one day do.

The anointing of Saul is a dramatic foreshadowing to the Wedding Supper of the Lamb that awaits us in the *high place of Heaven* in the Father's house. There we shall be brought into the hall, seated at the head table, and will enjoy a specially prepared meal with our High-Priest and Kingly Bridegroom Jesus, along with some specially invited guests.

After dining, Saul *descended* the high place with Samuel, and there was anointed with oil, kissed, and officially declared leader over His inheritance. This ceremony suggests the blue-print of the day every believer in Christ will be installed to co-reign on the earth beside her Eternal Husband, as destined in Revelation 5:10, "You have made them to be a kingdom and priests to serve our God, and they will reign on the earth."

CHAPTER 10 REFLECTION

1. Think of the *spiritual clothes* you dress yourself with every morning. Are they your own street clothes or the righteous robes of Christ?

2. With whom in the Bride-Church do you look forward to standing under Christ's bridal tent with? Write down their names.

3. Write down the names of those you know who have not yet accepted the King's invitation to attend the Wedding Supper of the Lamb. Commit to pray for them on a regular basis. Share God's love with them in some tangible way.

THE REIGN OF JESUS ON THE EARTH

"Do I take any pleasure in the death of the wicked?" declares the Sovereign
LORD. "Rather, am I not pleased when they turn from their ways and
live?" – Ezekiel 18:23

LAST CALL INVITATIONS

E ven as the Bride-Church is raptured safely up to Heaven,
still our merciful God wants none to perish. It is His
desire that all should come to a saving faith in Christ before He
comes a second time to the earth to pour out God's wrath.
Therefore, God will send *Two Witnesses* who will appear in
Jerusalem during the time of the Great Tribulation to preach
the Gospel to an unrepentant world.[1]

In Malachi 4:5, God said He will send "the prophet Elijah
to you *before* that great and dreadful day of the LORD comes."
Although Scripture records that John the Baptist came in the
spirit of Elijah and served as a herald for Messiah in Jesus's First
Coming, when asked if he *was* Elijah, he responded that he
was not.[2] So, what does this mean? It means the prophet Elijah
himself is coming again! And when Elijah returns, he will

come as herald to warn people of Jesus's Second Coming—calling all to repentance and faith. Some speculate that the Two Witnesses will be Elijah and Moses (both of whom appeared with Jesus on the Mount of Transfiguration) or Elijah and Enoch (both of whom did not physically die—but were taken up to Heaven by God). Whoever God chooses, they will prophesy and give testimony of salvation through Yeshua (Jesus) during the final three and a half years of the Tribulation, when Antichrist rules.

Some people who missed the Rapture of the Bride-Church will come to their senses and respond to the preaching of these Two Witnesses. These post-Rapture believers will do *anything* to be saved. This will mean martyrdom for their newly found faith in the LORD by not worshipping the beast (Antichrist) or his image, nor taking his mark on their forehead or hand in order to buy or sell. At the conclusion of their preaching assignment, the Two Witnesses will be killed by Antichrist and left on display for those in the kingdom of darkness to gloat over and celebrate. However, after three and a half days, the Two Witnesses will rise up to Heaven in a cloud—in full view of their enemies.[3]

Also, before the Second Coming of Jesus, God will send an angel with *one final Gospel invitation* to be publicly broadcast to all inhabitants who remain on the earth. In Revelation 14:6-7, the final call is recorded by the Apostle John:

> *I saw another angel flying in midair, and he had the eternal gospel to proclaim to those who live on the earth—to every nation, tribe, language, and people. He said in a loud voice, "Fear God, and give Him glory, because the hour of His judgment has come. Worship Him who made the Heaven, the earth, the sea and the springs of waters."*

With heightened alarm, this last-call invitation will carry the strongest of warnings against taking the mark of the beast, which seals each bearer's fate—banning their entrance into Heaven.[4] This worldwide appeal to bid all to come into the Kingdom of God while there is still time stands in stark contrast to the alternative of refusing God's salvation through Christ to remain in the kingdom of darkness. As described in Revelation 14:9-11a, those who choose to worship the beast of Antichrist over God will be bound and suffer everlasting torment:

> *A third angel followed them and said in a loud voice: "If anyone worships the beast and its image and receives its mark on their forehead or on their hand, they, too, will drink the wine of God's fury, which has been poured full strength into the cup of His wrath. They will be tormented with burning sulfur in the presence of the holy angels and of the Lamb. And the smoke of their torment will rise for ever and ever."*

But those who express their devotion to Christ through the ultimate sacrifice of martyrdom will be eternally rewarded. In Matthew 16:25-27, Jesus taught:

> *For whoever wants to save his life will lose it, but whoever loses their life for me will find it ... For the Son of Man is going to come in his Father's glory with his angels, and then he will reward each person according to what he has done.*

If you're feeling at all overwhelmed by these End Times events, remember the Book of Revelation was written to bless the reader and to provide encouragement that our LORD and Savior Jesus Christ will rescue all who turn to Him. He is the victorious One who defeats every enemy! As He reminds us throughout Revelation, those who belong to Him need not be afraid!

JESUS'S SECOND COMING

The Second Coming of the Lord Jesus Christ will occur at the end of the seven-year Tribulation period. Whereas the Rapture of the Bride-Church will be experienced only by believers, the Second Coming will be experienced worldwide. On that Day when Jesus touches back down on the earth, He will be accompanied by His angelic armies and His raptured Bride-Church. Although the rebellious nations will gather against Him on the battlefield of Armageddon, Jesus will soundly defeat them with the very breath of His mouth. As He treads the winepress of the wrath of God alone, His Bride will stand as a witness against them. Her clean, linen garments will not be soiled.[5]

The Apostle John was given a breathtaking prophetic vision in Revelation describing Jesus's Second Coming this way:

> *I saw Heaven standing open and there before me was a white horse, whose rider is called Faithful and True. With justice He judges and wages war. His eyes are like blazing fire, and on His head are many crowns ... He is dressed in a robe dipped in blood, and His name is the Word of God. The armies in Heaven were following Him, riding on white horses and dressed in fine linen white and clean. Coming out of his mouth is a sharp sword with which to strike down the nations. "He will rule them with an iron scepter." He treads the winepress of the fury of the wrath of God Almighty. On His robe and on his thigh He has this name written:*
>
> *KING OF KINGS AND LORD OF LORDS.* — Revelation 19:11-16

When Jesus returns as the triumphant Warrior King of Kings, a sweeping victory against the powerful forces of darkness will come to an astonishing closure. They are no match for Him!

... Then I saw the beast and the kings of the earth and their armies gathered together to make war against the rider on the horse and His army. But the beast was captured, and with it the false prophet who had performed the miraculous signs on its behalf ... The two of them were thrown alive into the fiery lake of burning sulfur. The rest of them were killed with the sword coming out of the mouth of the rider on the horse, and all the birds gorged themselves on their flesh. — Revelation 19:19-21

Just as God spoke the earth and its inhabitants into being, so too will Jesus defeat His enemies with the very breath of His mouth. With one word—they will all be finished! The righteous will rejoice, and the earth will once again flourish. As Jesus takes His glorious reign upon the earth with His Bride-Church ruling beside Him, it will usher in a new time of jubilant celebration, where righteousness will reign forever!

THE THOUSAND YEAR REIGN

Jesus's Second Coming will establish a time of unprecedented peace upon the earth where He will reign over His worldwide Kingdom with the Bride-Church at His side. As all evil will be banished, the redeemed citizens of Christ's marvelous Kingdom will include several groups of people who have been saved and are welcomed in. We can look forward to seeing a diverse multitude of people from every nation, tribe and language who secured their entrance into the Kingdom at varied points in the seven-year Tribulation timeline.

The first of these groups are members of the Bride-Church *and* the 144,000 Jewish believers. As presented earlier, both are described in the Bible as *firstfruits* to God.[6] Firstfruits because these were the first ones who put their faith in Jesus as their Savior and Lord and were marked by the Holy Spirit. Both groups will be kept safe from Antichrist through the time of the

Great Tribulation. The Bride-Church will be raised up to Heaven at the Splendid Day of the Rapture, while the 144,000 will remained on the earth during that time but be marked by God and left unharmed.

The second group we can look forward to seeing present in the Millennial reign of Jesus will be Jewish and Gentile people who missed the Rapture but came to a repentant faith in Christ while suffering through the Great Tribulation. This group are also considered as fruit of the earth. They are described as *a second crop* that will be harvested from Abraham's same spiritual family tree of faith—as are the Bride-Church and the 144,000. Amos 7:1 reveals what God plans "after the king's share had been harvested and just as the second crop was coming up." This scene connects to Revelation 9:3-4. Although not raptured up in the first harvest but coming to faith during the Great Tribulation, these post-Rapture saints will certainly be welcomed into the eternal Kingdom of God.

The post-Rapture saints are a unique group of people. A great majority of these believers will be Jewish, for God will remove the scales from their eyes so that they will see that Yeshua (Jesus) has been their Messiah all along. Zechariah 12:10 the LORD says, "And I will pour out on the house of David and the inhabitants of Jerusalem a spirit of grace and supplication. They will look on me, the one they have pierced, and they will mourn for him as one mourns for an only child."

As addressed earlier in this book, because the Jewish nation did not recognize Yeshua as their Messiah when He first came, they experienced a hardening of heart until the full number of Gentiles came to faith. However, there's good news! God will keep His covenant to Israel to ensure that a remnant from every tribe will be saved.[7] Because they miss the Rapture, they will suffer greatly under the 42-month rule and wrath of Antichrist. Zechariah 13:8-9 prophesies the staggering death toll that will take place. Staying true to the LORD will cost one's life. Even so, God will place a protective limit and bring the remnant through the fiery trial as gold. The Apostle John writes in Revelation 20:4 that they will come to life and reign with Christ a thousand years. Praise God for His love and restoration of those who fully devote themselves to Him!

THE GREAT FEAST ON THE EARTH

After Jesus establishes His Millennial reign on the earth, there will be a special celebration that the redeemed can look forward to. Our Lord is planning an incredible banquet where believers will publicly commune with Him at a table on the earth along with some other distinguished guests. This feast will not be hosted by the Father, but the Son.

It is likely that this event will be the first time the annual *Lord's Feast of Tabernacles*[8] (also known as the *Feast of Ingathering* or simply *the* feast) is observed after Jesus returns.[9] Deuteronomy 16:13 is a lasting ordinance that requires God's people to celebrate the *wheat* and *grape harvests* every year. This joyful feast will be carried into the Millennial Kingdom and observed as an annual celebration to remember God's bountiful provision and miraculous deliverance from the wicked!

The *Wheat Harvest* symbolizes the body of true believers who will be gathered from God's spiritual threshing floor and brought safely into His barn (while the weeds of counterfeit believers will be tied up to be later burned).[10] The *Grape Harvest* symbolizes the rotten grapes of evil who will be thrown into the winepress of God's wrath to be crushed under Jesus's feet.[11] [12]

Recorded in Luke 14:15-24, Jesus spoke of His future post-harvest banquet in telling the *Parable of the Great Feast* while dining at the house of a prominent Pharisee. Although His parable reads similar to the Parable of the Wedding Feast in Matthew 22:1-14, the Great Feast story does not harmonize with any of the other Gospels. It stands alone and speaks of the tremendous celebratory meal Jesus will hold when He returns to the earth.

Although both hosts in the two parables have disloyal invitees and direct their servants to extend the invitation to complete strangers, there are two distinguishing elements of Jesus's Parable of the Great Feast—namely, the *host* and the *location*.

The first distinguishing element is that the host who extends the invitation to the Great Feast is not the kingly father of the bridegroom, but a certain man. The Greek word *certain man* is the *same term* Jesus favored using whenever He referred to Himself as—the *Son of Man*.[13]

The second distinguishing element is the location of the banquet. It is not the same Greek word used for the tented heavenly bridal chamber or *wedding hall*[14] in Matthew 22, but rather the man's own inhabited house or palace on the earth.[15] In both the Old and New Testaments, the physical location of Mount Zion in Jerusalem where the Temple once stood was designated as the LORD's house.[16]

It is notable that just before Jesus tells the Parable of the Great Feast at the Pharisee's house, He observed how guests were picking the places of honor at the table. Using this opportunity to set the stage, He told a preceding parable about a *wedding feast* and the diversity of guests that will be present. Luke 14:8-11 records Jesus's teaching:

> *"When someone invites you to a wedding feast, do not take the place of honor, for a person more distinguished than you may have been invited. If so, the host who invited both of you will come and say to you, 'Give this man your seat.' Then, humiliated, you will have to take the least important place ... For all those who exalt themselves will be humbled, and those who humble themselves will be exalted."*

In this teaching, Jesus artfully reveals that the coming Great Feast on the earth will include all believers of every walk of life —from those less known to those well-known—such as Abraham, Isaac, Jacob, Daniel[17] and all the prophets. Luke 13:28-30 records Jesus's teaching about where the Great Feast will be held:

> *"There will be weeping there, and gnashing of teeth, when you (the unredeemed) see Abraham, Isaac and Jacob and all the prophets in the kingdom of God, but you yourselves thrown out. People will come from east and west and north and south, and will take their places at the feast in the kingdom of God. Indeed there are those who are last who will be first, and first who will be last."*

The fact that Jesus included details about the patriarchs and prophets as well as included the cardinal compass points of east, west, north, and south is significant. Jesus tells us that this special meal will occur on the earth, not in Heaven. Compass points do not apply in outer space.

Like any attentive banquet host, Jesus Himself will wait on His guests to make sure they are enjoying themselves! All in attendance will be lavishly blessed—just read what Isaiah 25:6 tells us—"On this mountain the LORD Almighty will prepare a feast of rich food for all peoples, a banquet of aged wine—the best of meats and the finest of wines."

GREAT EXPECTATIONS

> *Now when Jesus returned, a crowd welcomed Him, for they were all expecting Him.* — Luke 8:4

And so, it will be that those who miss the Rapture but give their hearts to Jesus during the Great Tribulation (and manage to stay alive) will wait in *great expectation* for Christ's Second Coming and the tremendous blessings that will follow. For those who find themselves left behind, Jesus encourages them with these words:

> *Be dressed ready for service and keep your lamps burning, like servants waiting for their master to return from a wedding banquet, so that when he comes and knocks they can immediately open the door for him. It will be good for those servants whose master finds them watching when he comes. Truly I tell you, he will dress himself to serve, will have them recline at the table and will come and wait on them.* — Luke 12:35-37

Daniel 12 and Revelation 13 provide three *Save the Date Notices* for the Messianic events to take place on the earth when Jesus returns. These exact dates will not be calculable until the future *abomination of desolation* by Antichrist takes place at the halfway point of the seven-year Tribulation. The new believers who come to Christ after the Rapture will be able to console themselves by counting forward 1260, 1290, and 1335 days, respectively, to reach the end of evil's rule, the beginning of the restoration of the earth, and the celebration of the Great Feast with the Lord Jesus in His Millennial Kingdom. To wait for these events to take place will call for patient endurance and faithfulness on the part of God's people. [18]

SHEEP AND GOAT JUDGMENT

Those who will be welcomed into the Millennial Kingdom of Christ and present at the Great Feast on the earth will be members of His Bride-Church who were raptured, believers who came to faith during the Great Tribulation but were martyred and came back to life[19], and Old Testament distinguished guests. Additionally, there will be some unassuming guests who will be surprised to learn that they, too, have gained entrance. The Bible teaches that there will be *survivors* who live through the Great Tribulation—an incredible example of God's mercy and grace! Joel 2:32 provides this truth, "And everyone who calls on the name of the LORD will be saved; for on Mt. Zion and in Jerusalem there will be deliverance, as the LORD has said, even among the survivors, whom the LORD has called."

These Great Tribulation survivors—who remarkably remain alive—are people from every nation who demonstrated their fear and belief in God in tangible ways by taking care of Jesus's followers who are in desperate need. In the Old Testament, the prostitute Rahab did the same thing for the two Israelite spies—hiding them from those who were hunting them down. Acknowledging the miracles of God and how her heart melted in fear of the LORD, she confessed her faith by saying, "the LORD your God is God in Heaven above and on the earth below."

Rahab's profession of faith in the Lord saved her, and her kind actions toward the people of God confirmed her faith was true.[20] As a result, Rahab was kept safe through the Battle of Jericho and welcomed as an honored member into the community of God!

Just like Rahab, there will be some in the Last Days who will be far away from Jesus but will turn to Him as their hearts melt in fear by the miracles, signs and wonders of God they see and experience. Indeed—Revelation 11:13 says that there will be a severe earthquake which will cause survivors to be terrified and give glory to the God of Heaven!

As King Jesus sits on His glorious throne in Jerusalem to begin His Millennial reign, all the survivors of the nations will be gathered before Him. At that time, He will separate the people one from another as a shepherd separates the sheep from the goats. This event is referred to as the *Sheep and Goat*

Judgment in Matthew 25:31-46. The *sheep* will be placed on His right and the *goats* on His left. The sheep will gain entrance into the Millennial Kingdom and attend the Great Feast as welcomed guests. As Rahab did, these people professed faith in the Lord Jesus and tangibly demonstrated their fear of God by showing kindness to His people during the Great Tribulation by feeding, clothing, caring, and protecting them.

Not so the unbelieving goats. They did not profess faith in Jesus and heartlessly turned their backs on God's people by not extending any kindness nor help when needed. Because their actions demonstrated their lack of fear of God, King Jesus will pronounce judgement on them. The goats will be forever exiled from the earth and cast into eternal punishment.

RESTORATION OF THE EARTH

> *For the creation waits in eager expectation for the children of God to be revealed. For the creation was subjected to frustration, not by its own choice, but by the will of the one who subjected it, in hope that the creation itself will be liberated from its bondage to decay and brought into the glorious freedom of the children of God.* — Romans 8:19-21

Almost complete destruction will come upon the earth during the time of the seven-year Tribulation with earthquakes, fire, hail, the battle of Armageddon, and the final fall of Babylon—the evil world system of the Last Days.[21] After this, not much will remain. However, by God's goodness—renewal and beauty will be reestablished upon the earth.

The Bible gives a wondrous picture of what the world will look like once paradise lost becomes paradise *restored*. Isaiah describes the refreshing of the land:

The desert and the parched land will be glad; the wilderness will rejoice and blossom... it will burst into bloom; it will rejoice greatly and shout for joy... they will see the glory of the LORD, the splendor of our God... Then will the eyes of the blind be opened and the ears of the deaf unstopped. Then will the lame leap like a deer, and the mute tongue shout for joy. Water will gush forth in the wilderness and streams in the desert. — Isaiah 35:1-2, 5-6

In addition to the restoration of the land, Isaiah also speaks of what life will be like for those who *live* in the land. God offers a picture of hope and blessing unlike anything seen on the earth before:

Never again will there be in it an infant who lives but a few days, or an old man who does not live out his years ... They will build houses and dwell in them; they will plant vineyards and eat their fruit ... For as the days of a tree, so will be the days of my people; my chosen ones will long enjoy the work of their hands. They will not labor in vain, nor will they bear children doomed to misfortune; for they will be a people blessed by the LORD, they and their descendants with them. — Isaiah 65:20-23

What an incredible vision we are given here! While we may be experiencing challenges on the earth today, one day in the future—all our sorrows will be a distant memory.

CO-REIGNING IN THE KINGDOM

Once the King of Kings establishes His reign upon the earth, the believer's new life and status will carry one of the highest privileges of role and service. Granted sovereignty, power, and greatness, believers will serve as judges with authority over the nations, co-reigning beside Him.[22]

Crowns are widely known as iconic symbols of royalty,

victory, and reward. There are also crowns of scorn and shame, of which Christ once wore on our behalf. However, when Jesus returns to the earth, He will don many magnificent crowns.[23] Isaiah 28:5 exudes that He "will be a glorious crown, a beautiful wreath for the remnant of His people."

As fitting in any royal coronation where the high priest is the one who bestows the crown, our High Priestly King Jesus will determine which crowns each of His beloved will receive. The following outlines the various crowns:

1. The *Crown of Righteousness* for those eager for Christ's return (2 Timothy 4:7-8)
2. The *Crown of Life* for those who persevere under trial (James 1:12)
3. The *Crown of Joy* for those we bring to Christ (1 Thessalonians 2:19)
4. The *Incorruptible Crown* for those who run with focus and passion (1 Corinthians 9:25)
5. The *Crown of Victory* for those who run in accordance with God's Word (2 Timothy 2:5)
6. The *Crown of Beauty* for the brokenhearted (Isaiah 61:3)
7. The *Crown of Glory* for those who care for God's people (1 Peter 5:2-4)
8. The *Crown of Splendor* for the New Jerusalem (Isaiah 62:3-5)

Note: Crowns will one day be laid at Jesus's feet—the only One truly worthy.[24]

THE NEW JERUSALEM

Christ's Millennial reign will occur on the earth as we presently know it. When the thousand years are over, the heavens and earth will be purified by fire and then recreated and presented in a stunningly dramatic way.[25] The culmination of where we will ultimately spend eternity will be a place God creates that *no eye has ever seen, nor ear has ever heard, nor mind has conceived.*[26]

John gives us a glimpse of our future home as revealed to him in a vision:

Then I saw "'a new Heaven and a new earth," for the first Heaven and the first earth had passed away... I saw the Holy City, the new Jerusalem, coming down out of Heaven from God, prepared as a bride beautifully dressed for her husband. And I heard a loud voice from the throne saying, "Look! God's dwelling place is now among the people, and He will dwell with them. They will be His people, and God Himself will be with them and be their God. He will wipe every tear from their eyes. There will be no more death or mourning or crying or pain, for the old order of things has passed away." — Revelation 21:1-4*

John goes on to reveal the dazzling city of the New Jerusalem as the *bride, the wife of the Lamb:*

One of the seven angels ... said ..., "Come, I will show you the bride, the wife of the Lamb." And he carried me away in the Spirit ... and showed me the Holy City, Jerusalem, coming down out of Heaven from God. It shone with the glory of God, and its brilliance was like that of a very precious jewel... clear as crystal. — Revelation 21:9-11

You may ask, "How can this celestial city be the bride?" The simple answer is that the essence of every city is the people who dwell there. In Revelation 3:12, Jesus said, "The one who is victorious I will make a pillar in the temple of My God." Obviously, we won't be turned into cold stone structures, but we will be as living stones—built together as a spiritual house with Jesus as the Chief Cornerstone.[27]

No longer separated, Heaven and earth will wondrously intersect. This dazzling home will be a physical place in time and space with a size beyond comprehension. Much more than a showplace, it will exist as a dynamic and vibrant reflection of God's holiness and glorious light!

CHAPTER 11 REFLECTION

1. Which Old Testament prophet or person do you look forward to meeting at the Great Feast on the earth and why?

2. For which crowns do you believe you currently qualify for?

3. Are there any crowns you would like to add to your list? Which ones?

4. Which crown do you find the most difficult to attain? Ask the Holy Spirit to help you attain it.

5. What aspect of your Eternal Home are you most excited about?

PART 4: WHAT TO DO WHILE YOU WAIT

ARISE AND SHINE

Arise, shine, for your light has come, and the glory of the LORD rises upon you. See, darkness covers the earth and thick darkness is over the peoples, but the LORD rises upon you and His glory appears over you. Nations will come to your light, and kings to the brightness of your dawn ... Then you will look and be radiant, your heart will throb and swell with joy. –
Isaiah 60:1-3,5a

We have learned that a perfect match made in Heaven has been pre-arranged by the Heavenly Father for His Son, Jesus Christ. His betrothed Bride is composed of members of His worldwide Church throughout the ages who have accepted Jesus's proposal of love and entered the everlasting covenant with Him by accepting the bride-price of Jesus's shed blood as payment for their sins. The picture of a husband and wife is used throughout Scripture to describe this mysteriously beautiful union—a union where God's choice and man's free will intersect.

The parallels between a first-century Hebrew wedding and

the coming of Jesus to rapture His Bride-Church help us understand the order of Last Days events. In biblical days, only the groom's father knew the exact day and time when the bridegroom would arrive. However, the bride always had a general sense of the approaching time. While watching for the bridegroom in great anticipation, she would remain watchful, preparing herself for that day.

So too, does our Heavenly Father know the exact day and time when His Son Jesus will arrive for His Bride, the Church. While we are not privy to the precise time of Christ's return, we await that Splendid Day, knowing God keeps His promises. Christ will come! And so, we eagerly await His coming— remaining watchful and preparing our hearts for that day.

This book has provided in-depth steps for you to do just that. Take those steps now and you will be forever grateful. With your wedding garments cleaned and pressed, your face unveiled, and your oil lamp filled, you will achieve an inner and outer radiance, making you confident and ready to meet the heavenly Bridegroom when He comes.

Since the beginning of the Church Age, each generation of the faithful have wondered if their generation might be the one to see that Splendid Day of the Rapture arrive. Guess what? There is much biblical evidence that suggests we may be that generation! Without looking at the headline news, we turn to the Bible.

SIGNIFICANCE OF THE THIRD DAY

There is great significance regarding astounding happenings *on the third day* weaved throughout Scripture. The "third day" is often referred to as *a day of double-blessing* as a reading of Genesis 1:9-13 reveals. It is the only day in the story of creation where God *twice* pronounces it "good". The most widely recognized third day event is the day Jesus miraculously rose from the dead! However, there are other third day references that are worthy of our attention as we anticipate the day of the Rapture of the Bride-Church.

CONSIDER THESE THIRD DAY EVENTS:

1. *On the third day* the Israelites were to be consecrated, wash their clothes, and be ready for the Lord to come down in the sight of all His people. —Exodus 19:10-11
2. *On the third day* there was thunder, lightning, a thick cloud, and a very loud trumpet blast. Then Moses led the people out to meet with God. —Exodus 19:16-17
3. *On the third day* God promises to restore us that we may live in His presence. —Hosea 6:2
4. On the *third day* the restored Temple was completed. —Ezra 6:15
5. On the *third day* Queen Esther "put on her royal robes and stood in the inner court of the palace, in front of the king's hall." —Esther 5:1
6. *On the third day*, Jesus said He would reach His goal. —Luke 13:32
7. On the *third day* a wedding took place in Cana where Jesus revealed His glory. —John 2:1
8. On the *third day,* God raised Jesus from the dead and caused Him to be seen. —Acts 10:40

God's record of keeping time is not like ours, for "With the Lord a day is like a thousand years, and a thousand years are like a day" (2 Peter 3:8). Applying this divine mathematical conversion, Jesus was crucified more than 2,000 years ago, or just over two "God-days" ago. This would mean that according to the prophetic timeline, the world's calendar is currently *early into the third day.*

Over two God-days ago, Jesus secured salvation when He took the sins of the world upon Himself on the cross at Calvary and imparted His righteousness to all who would put their faith in Him. Thereafter, human history entered a third God-day where the redeemed are promised to live again in God's presence in paradise, as Adam and Eve once did in the Garden of Eden.

Besides the recognition that we are living early in the third day, there are current events in the world that are considered fulfillments of End Times prophecies. If you haven't been paying attention, it's time. Jesus said in Luke 21 that there will be signs in the sun, moon, stars, and earth that will indicate the time of His return—for "when these things begin to take place, stand up and lift up your heads, because your redemption is drawing near" (Luke 21:28).

Romans 13:11-12 tells us, "And do this, understand the present time: The hour has already come for you to wake up from your slumber, because our salvation is nearer now than when we first believed. The night is nearly over; the day is almost here."

Understanding the present times and exploring the myriad of signs and wonders that indicate that the time for Jesus to return is upon us is beyond the scope of this book. However, I encourage you to do your homework. Evidence abounds!

Approximately 30 percent of the Bible is prophetic. There are excellent articles and books written to help open your eyes to see that the time for the Rapture of the Bride-Church and Christ's Second Coming is close. Author and Pastor Jimmy Evans said in his book *"Tipping Point—The End is Here"* that, "When Jesus returns and the end comes, no person on the planet will have an excuse for not being ready."[1]

Should you wish to do further study on this subject,

Matthew 24, Mark 13, Luke 17:20-37, and Luke 21 are passages that give detailed descriptions of the prophetic road signs we can watch for that will precede both the Rapture of the Bride-Church and Christ's Second Coming to the earth.

THE RADIANCE OF GOD'S GLORY

At the beginning of this book, I shared that the day Joseph and I married is October 20th. As was mentioned, the spiritual application of this date is that it is believed by some to mark the appearance of the Bethlehem star announcing the birth of Jesus. Whether it is the correct date or not is inconsequential, however the appearance of the Bethlehem star conveys the idea that as the faithful commit our lives to the Light of the World—Jesus, we become carriers of His light.

Hebrews 1:3 states that Jesus "is the radiance of God's glory and the exact representation of His being." Likewise, you and I are also destined to brilliantly reflect Christ to the world. Each one of us are called to let our light so shine in a way that others can see the good things we do that will bring praise to God in Heaven.[2]

When Christ was gloriously transfigured before three of His disciples, "His face shone like the sun, and His clothes became as white as the light" (Matthew 17:1-2). This special revelation was given so every follower of Christ could better understand Jesus's divinity and the transformation that awaits *us*—so that we too can shine brightly in a dark world. The Apostle Peter recounted this scene as:

> ... *eyewitnesses of His Majesty. He received honor and glory from God the Father when the voice came to Him from the Majestic Glory, saying, "This is my Son, whom I love; with Him I am well pleased." We ourselves heard this voice ... and you will do well to pay attention to it, as to a light shining in a dark place, until the day*

dawns and the morning star rises in your hearts. — 2 Peter 1:16b-19

THE BRIGHT MORNING STAR

The name Jesus last called Himself in the Bible was the *bright Morning Star.*[3] If you look up into the heavens in the early hours just before dawn breaks, against the dark sky you can see stars twinkling their brightest. Jesus gave every believer a Great Commission to "go and make disciples of all nations, baptizing them in the name of the Father and of the Son and of the Holy Spirit, and teaching them to obey everything I have commanded you" (Matthew 28:19-20).

Together as the Bride-Church acts to fulfill this commission, we release His light into a spiritually needy world. The prophet Daniel used the same illustration when he said, "Those who are wise will shine like the brightness of the heavens, and those who lead many to righteousness, like the stars for ever and ever" (Daniel 12:3). All believers in the Lord Jesus Christ, both Jewish and Gentile, together fulfill the ancient covenant God made to Abraham that one day his descendants would be as numerous as the stars in the sky.

SHOWERED WITH GIFTS FROM ABOVE

"Well and good," you may say. "But just how do I shine my light to help fulfill the Great Commission?" For some, evangelism comes easy, but for others it can be daunting. I'll share a secret—*just use whatever you have.* A tangible example of this is evident when Jesus feeds the five thousand with meager fish and loaves. The multitudes were tired and hungry. The disciples thought it best to send them away to forage for their own food. But Jesus corrected their thinking, and instead asked them, *"What do you have?"* Presenting a few fish and some bread to Him, Jesus blessed it, giving thanks, and it miraculously multiplied to feed thousands. Little is much in God's economy.[4] In this way, He receives the glory. So, what do you have? Let's look...

God has an enormous charitable heart. All three of the Godhead—God the Father, the Son, and the Holy Spirit, are involved in the distribution of gifts. First Corinthians 12:4-6 tells us, "There are different kinds of gifts, but the same Spirit distributes them. There are different kinds of service, but the same Lord. There are different kinds of working, but in all of them and in everyone it is the same God at work."

Gifts are birthed in the heart of the Father and are hand-selected for every human being. As it is written, "Every good and perfect gift is from above, coming down from the Father of the heavenly lights" (James 1:17).

Certainly, life and faith are gifts from God. However, there are other gifts the Father gives us from birth in which we will naturally excel. These gifts include prophecy, serving, teaching, encouraging, giving, leadership, and mercy. These gifts and the calling you will receive from God to use them are irrevocable.[5]

Gifts will usually manifest at an early age. As a child, I had a desire to teach. It came naturally, so I would often play school with my siblings and neighborhood kids. What was my favorite role-play? Teaching in front of the class, of course! Later in life, I would become a professor at a local community college teaching computer science. Unbeknownst to me, during this time my gift was being developed. However, using my God-given gift for *purely* secular purposes was not my true calling. There is a difference.

Once you recognize the natural gifts you have been given from the Father, you will do well in life to commit their use in a way that will honor Him. Serving in your local church or ministry where opportunities present themselves is one way to appropriate your gifts. However, using them as a witness in the secular marketplace or other avenues where you work is just as impactful and, frankly, where most evangelism takes place.

Jesus will open doors for where you are to use your gifts. As you follow His lead and walk through those doors, you will discover great fulfillment! Whether it be in a corner office on Wall Street or a school cafeteria, every one of us is needed to do our part if we are to reach the world. Not only does Jesus determine *who* will be his apostles, prophets, evangelists, pastors, or teachers in various places, but He will also *equip* you for wherever He may send you.[6]

After teaching nine years in the community college system, one day Jesus closed that door and opened a new door for me to begin using my gift for His glory. It was a calling that gave me the amazing privilege to teach His Word in Community Bible Study, as well as in other church ministries. I've been doing this work for 30 years and counting, and I have seen uncountable numbers of lives changed, healed, and strengthened for the Kingdom of God.

Wherever He sends me, all I do is show up with my few fish and loaves, thank Him for the privilege, and He somehow blesses and multiplies it—distributing His truth and grace to the tired and hungry. My husband, Joseph, has a similar calling and privilege. Both of us simply use what we have, and you can too!

Just as the Father selects the gifts and the Son determines the calling, the Spirit will actively choose through whom He will distribute gifts to those in need. It is exhilarating to be used by God as His instrument to touch another person's life. The Holy Spirit can certainly work apart from us, but He often works through us—if we allow Him.

The gifts the Holy Spirit imparts for the common good are listed as wisdom, knowledge, faith, healing, miracles, prophecy, discernment, tongues and interpretation of tongues.[7] As Pastor Jack Hayford explains, "Jesus gives us the gift of the Holy

Spirit, yet when the Spirit comes, He is loaded with packages! He desires to release much more in us and through us than we could ever imagine. These gifts are given for delivery, not for accumulation. We receive them to pass them on to others."[8]

SHINING AS STARS IN THE UNIVERSE

In Philippians 2:13-16, we are reminded:

> *It is God who works in you to will and act in order to fulfill His good purpose. Do everything without grumbling or arguing, so that you may become blameless and pure, "children of God without fault in a warped and crooked generation." Then you will shine among them like stars in the sky as you hold firmly to the Word of life.*

The Holy Spirit is the One who raised Jesus from the dead, healed the sick, cast out demons, makes the weak strong, gives the repentant faith to believe, and causes the light of Jesus to shine in and through us to reach others. This gives us great confidence as we partner with Him.

Ephesians 2:10 is an exciting verse that tells us that God has planned good works for each one of us to do for His glory! Just read the promise and consider what it is He is calling you to do. Paul writes, "For we are God's handiwork, created in Christ Jesus to do good works, which God prepared in advance for us to do."

When you step into that specially prepared place arranged just for you, you will know in your heart that this is what you were made to do all along! Using your gifts for God's purposes brings not only joy, but also great fulfillment in life.

A WITNESS IN THE SKY

"...it will be established forever like the moon, the faithful witness in the sky." — Psalm 89:37

WHAT WE SPEAK IS IMPORTANT. We must open our mouth and testify about Jesus in a manner so that others can hear and choose to believe. Faith comes to someone when they *hear* the Word of God.[9] This is not always easy to do, but it's what we're asked to do. What the hearers do with the Gospel is their responsibility. We just need to make sure we follow through with ours. Opportunities to share abound. If you pray for one, it will soon present itself.

One of my favorite places to bear witness of Jesus is on an airplane. The audience is captive, and there are few interruptions. One day I prayed for an opportunity, and I sure got one! It was on a coast-to-coast flight across the United States where I was seated next to an electrical engineer who I will call Bart. Bart was a devout atheist.

Our conversation began when we pulled out our reading material. I pulled out my Bible and Bart pulled out his *Scientific American* magazine, and we went from there. We had almost five hours together, and I can tell you that I needed every minute of those hours, because he was a tough one! I was thankful though, because Bart challenged my faith and knowledge of the Word, and I could tell that he enjoyed the conversation too.

Before we engaged in our theological discussion, we laid some ground rules. He said he was afraid he'd offend me. I told him that if he spoke as a gentleman, I would not get offended. He hesitated and then looking directly in my eyes, he warned me that the last time he challenged a Christian about his faith, that person abandoned his faith. I was taken aback, but I knew that God didn't sit me next to this man to remain silent.

As we began to reason with each other what surprised me the most was this man's knowledge of Scripture. He was firing off Bible verses faster than I could! It just amazed me. Because of his interest in science, we waded into the waters of evolution and creationism. I asked him to consider the evidence in archeology and the lack of transitional forms in the fossil record. We even discussed the Second Law of Thermodynamics.

Still, he was not convinced. I incorporated the Gospel at every opportune time, but he continued to reject the foundational truth that the Bible is the inspired Word of God written by the hand of men through the Holy Spirit.[10] This he could not accept.

Somewhere in the middle of our discussion I learned Bart had been called in on 9/11 to help restore power to the city of New York. I asked him how he was affected by that experience. He told me that on his drive home, he wrote a poem to release his emotions on paper. He conveniently had a copy of it in his briefcase and asked if I'd like to read it. I took the poem and began to read it very slowly and purposely, trying to better understand this man in order to reach him for Christ. I thanked him and handed the poem back, but Bart insisted I keep it. I thanked him again and tucked it into my bag.

About four hours into the conversation, we came to a point where Bart decided it was time to use his trump card, and I sensed in my Spirit that he was going in for the kill. He asked if I believed in *dualism*. It's the belief that everything has an opposite: good/evil, light/dark, positive/negative, matter/antimatter. But the thing with matter/antimatter is when matter meets its antimatter, the object disappears. It vanishes. You have nothing. I said, "Yes, I believe that."

Bart then took me through a series of reasoning starting with his glass of orange juice. He held it up and asked, "Mary, if this glass of orange juice suddenly met its antimatter what would you have?" I said, "Nothing. But you'd still have the airplane and all of the people on it."

He said, "Good, good. And if this airplane and all the people on it suddenly met its antimatter, what would you have?" I said, "Nothing. But you'd still have the world."

Delighted by my response, Bart again complimented me by saying, "Good. And if the world and everything in and on it suddenly met its antimatter, what would you have?" I said, "Nothing. But you'd still have the universe." To which Bart nodded.

Then he paused before asking me his final question —"Mary, if the universe and everything in it, every star, every galaxy, every single molecule met its antimatter, then what would you have?"

I responded simply, "God. You'd have God."

Bart jerked back, shook his head, and looked at me. Staring back, I gently added, "Bart, His name is *I AM*."[11] Suddenly Bart's eyes got all misty, as He softly replied, "That's beautiful! I have never heard that before. Everyone always says 'Nothing.'" I knew then that it was time to remain silent, and let the Holy Spirit do His work on this man's heart.

Feeling tired, I put my head back against my seat and tried to close my eyes. But as I sat there, the Holy Spirit prompted me that as Bart had given me a poem, I needed to give him one in return. By God's doing, I happened to have a copy of a poem my friend's 13-year-old daughter had written two weeks before she died—two days before she even fell ill. Her poem was titled "Eternal Life," and in it she talks about life, death, and the good news of Jesus Christ. I asked if he'd like to read it. He said he would. Bart carefully took the poem and read it very slowly, very thoughtfully. "That's beautiful," he said, noticeably shaken and choking back tears. I responded, "You see Bart, God really can speak through the pen of a man."

Bart was quiet for the remainder of the flight. Keeping the poem, he thanked me before we went our separate ways.

I prayed Bart would soon come to know Jesus. To this day I still don't know what happened to him. Perhaps I'll see Bart on the Heaven-bound flight of the Rapture, but the truth is that the eternal destiny of any soul is not up to us. That is the free will decision of each person. All we can do is ask God to use us and then share the love and good news of Jesus as opportunities arise.

ALL STARS HAVE PATHS

In the Heavens God has pitched a tent for the sun... it rises at one end of the Heavens and makes its circuit to the other. — Psalm 19:4,6

As we've reached the end of this book, my encouragement to you is don't be afraid to shine Christ's light with the people God puts in your path. That's why He puts them in *your* path, and not someone else's. I would have never guessed I was ready to share Jesus with someone like Bart, but the Holy Spirit was guiding me every step of the way. What I learned from that encounter is that God is preparing and equipping me for every good work.

This is true for you, as well. Whether you're a new believer or a seasoned one, a Bible scholar or in spiritual pre-school, with whatever you have, *it will be enough.* For me, God used the few fish and loaves I had to share with Bart. What happened? God was able to touch this man's heart with my limited knowledge of scientific proof that God exists, a steadfast faith, and a little girl's poem.[12]

The Lord won't give you more than you can handle, and as illustrated in my story, if it is needed, He will frustrate the intelligence of the intelligent.[13] With a promise like that, you won't be intellectually out maneuvered nor put to shame. Remember what 2 Corinthians 3:5 says, "Not that we are competent in ourselves to claim anything for ourselves, but our competence comes from God." It's time to believe it and act! This world is lost and offers no hope. We have the answer. It is Jesus! And we should boldly proclaim Him and His life-saving Gospel while there is still time.

As world economies and governments falter, as crime, disease, natural disasters, and moral depravity increase, people will become more and more desperate for rescue, peace, and hope. Some hearts will be hardened in the process, but others will soften and be open.

Though these last days are getting darker, it gives the perfect backdrop for the Church to rise and shine. As Russian novelist Fyodor Dostoyevsky famously wrote, "The darker the night, the brighter the stars, the deeper the grief, the closer is God!"[14] May this be the Church's brightest hour!

JESUS IS COMING SOON

Four times in Revelation Jesus said that He is coming *soon*.[15] In Greek the word *soon* means *shortly, without delay, suddenly, quickly.*[16] Consider the urgency of His words, and how the Church has never been closer to seeing the fruition of His prophetic promise.

"I am coming soon. Hold on to what you have, so that no one will take your crown." — Revelation 3:11

"Look, I am coming soon! Blessed is the one who keeps the words of the prophecy written in this scroll." — Revelation 22:7

"Look, I am coming soon! My reward is with Me, and I will give to each person according to what they have done." — Revelation 22:12

"He who testifies to these things says, 'Yes, I am coming soon.'" —
Revelation 22:20

READY OR NOT...

All awaited the arrival of *the bridegroom*. It had been a long, arduous year. For him to return now and whisk away his betrothed would mean that the celebration could finally begin. It was just what was needed, causing the tiny village to stir with anticipation.

Although not knowing exactly when the bridal festivities would commence, there was much chatter in the air that the time was right. A wedding always has a way of lifting the spirits of the invitees. There is something about two lives being joined in covenant that imparts hope and promise for the brighter future the human heart perpetually seeks.

Usually, a bridegroom would make his entrance around midnight, so illumination was essential. Mindful of what was needed, some villagers wisely readied themselves for the big event by securing the precious oil to fuel their lamps. Soon after—they dressed in their clean, pressed wedding garments and taking the oil along with their lamps, ventured outdoors to wait alongside the others. Due to the late hour, all succumbed to sleep.

Then, in the dead of the night, the trumpet sounded, and the grand announcement was made—the Bridegroom is here! Jolted from their slumber, the ones prepared with oil quickly trimmed their lamps. Gaining entrance into the glorious wedding feast was their sole ambition, and now the Splendid Day had come!

Faces cast with resplendent light—**before they knew it, they had left the ground** and suddenly ... they were THERE!

MARY SOLER

Will you be there?

The Bible ends with the unified voice of the Spirit and the Bride beckoning Jesus to "Come!" If you have put your faith in the Lord Jesus Christ and can join your voice to the impassioned call, then take heart—*YOU ARE READY!*

CHAPTER 12 REFLECTION

1. List any God-given gifts you have. If you don't know your spiritual gifts, ask someone who knows you well. (Hint: They bring a deep sense of fulfillment when they are used.)

2. Are you currently using your gifts to help fulfill the Great Commission? Why or why not? If not, ask the Lord to provide you opportunities to use them, and then do it!

3. Think about the person who led you to faith in Christ and write down their name(s). Take a moment to thank God for them. Now ask the Lord to use YOU to be that person to someone else in sharing God's love and the good news of the Gospel.

4. Spend some time praising your Eternal Husband. Thank Jesus for loving you and for His promise to return for you one day and take you where He is in Heaven!

PART 5: RESOURCES

APPENDIX A

THE SEVEN CHURCHES OF REVELATION

In Revelation chapters 1-3, Jesus is seen standing among seven golden lampstands, each representing one of His churches of various congregations around the world throughout the ages to today. As Jesus describes the spiritual state of each, five are noted as compromised. To these five churches Jesus acknowledges their good works, but He also gives a stern rebuke—calling them to repent.

Jesus fully commends only two of the seven churches with no correction. For all those in every church who overcome by walking faithfully before the Lord, many blessings are promised! The following pages provide a summary of the seven categories of churches.

EPHESUS—The Loveless Church (Revelation 2:1-7)

Praise: Jesus knows their good deeds, hard work, perseverance, intolerance of the wicked, and testing of those who call themselves apostles. They have endured hardships, not given themselves to weariness, and hate the practices of the Nicolaitans.

Rebuke: They have forsaken their first love—Jesus.

Warning: REPENT or your lampstand will be removed!

Promise to Overcomers: You will have the right to eat from Tree of Life in the paradise of God.

SMYRNA—*The Persecuted Church (Revelation 2:8-11)

Praise: Jesus knows their affliction and poverty, yet they are rich! They have been slandered by those who say they are Jews and are not but are a "synagogue of Satan." Some will be imprisoned as a test and suffer persecution for ten days.

Rebuke: NONE

Warning: Do not be afraid of what you are to suffer.

Promise to Overcomers: Be faithful even to the point of death, and they will be given the crown of life. They will not be hurt at all by the second death (Lake of Fire; Revelation 20:14).

PERGAMUM—The Compromising Church (Revelation 2:12-17)

Praise: Jesus knows where they live and that they remain true to His name. They did not renounce their faith in Him even when pressed.

Rebuke: Satan's throne has been set in you. Some hold to the teaching of Balaam who entice eating food sacrificed to idols and sexual immorality. Some also hold to the teaching of the Nicolaitans.

Warning: REPENT! Otherwise, Jesus will wage war against the evildoers with the sword of His mouth.

Promise to Overcomers: You will be given some of the hidden manna and a white stone with a new name written on it, known only to him who receives it.

THYATIRA—The Corrupt Church (Revelation 2:18-29)

Praise: Jesus knows their deeds of love, faith, service, perseverance, and that they are doing more than they did at first.

Rebuke: They tolerate the false prophetess Jezebel, whose teaching misleads God's servants into sexual immorality and idolatry. Jezebel is given time to repent, but she is unwilling and will be cast onto a bed of suffering. Her children will be stricken dead.

Warning: REPENT or suffer! Those who commit adultery with Jezebel will be thrown into great Tribulation unless they repent of their ways.

Promise to Overcomers: To those who do not follow Jezebel's teachings, hold on to what you have until Jesus comes. They will be given authority over the nations and the morning star.

SARDIS—The Dead Church (Revelation 3:1-6)

Praise: Jesus knows their deeds and their reputation of being alive. You have a few people who have not soiled their clothes.

Rebuke: They have a reputation of being alive, but they are actually dead! Their deeds are not complete in sight of God.

Warning: They are admonished to wake up! Strengthen what remains and is about to die. Remember what was received and heard. Obey it and REPENT! If they do not repent, Jesus will come like a thief, and they will not know the time that He will come!

Promise to Overcomers: They will be dressed in white and have a name that will never be blotted out from the book of life. Their name will be acknowledged before the Father and His angels.

PHILADELPHIA—*The Faithful Church (Revelation 3:7-13)

Praise: Jesus knows they have little strength but have kept God's Word and not denied His name. He will make the liars of the "synagogue of Satan" fall down at their feet and acknowledge that He loves them. They keep Jesus's command to endure patiently.

Rebuke: NONE

Warning: NONE

Promise to Overcomers: Since they kept Jesus's command to endure patiently, they will be kept from the hour of trial that is coming upon the whole world. They are to hold on so no one can take their crown. Jesus will make them a pillar in the temple of God. Never again will they leave it. They will have written on them the name of God, God's city (the New Jerusalem coming down out of Heaven) and Jesus's new name.

LAODICEA—The Lukewarm Church (Revelation 3:14-22)

Praise: None

Rebuke: Jesus knows their deeds—that they are neither hot nor cold, but lukewarm and about to be spit out of His mouth! They boast they are rich, but they are wretched, pitiful, poor, blind, and naked.

Warning: They are counseled to buy gold refined in the fire, to put on white clothes to cover their shameful nakedness, and to put salve on their eyes to see. Be earnest and REPENT! Jesus is at the door knocking. Open it, so He can come in and have a restored relationship with them.

Promise to Overcomers: Jesus will give the right to sit with Him on His throne, just as He overcame and sat down with His Father on His throne.

---

*FINAL NOTE

Smyrna and Philadelphia are the two churches that Jesus commends without finding any fault. Both churches drew fire and were harassed by the "synagogue of Satan."

The devil currently has a throne and place to live in spiritual Pergamum. He freely moves about the earth—"prowling around like a roaring lion looking for someone to devour" (1 Peter 5:8). However, one day Satan will be bound and thrown into the Lake of Fire forever, unable to attack God's people anymore. (See Revelation 20)

"Eternal Life"

by Hannah Davis written on December 12, 2003

I wrote this poem and placed it in a time capsule for the future
to read. I want to tell you of the Way, the Truth, and the Life.

When there is no place to go,
just look around and you'll know
that there must be something more.
Just look for the open door,
and in the doorway he will stand
with a multitude of angels from some distant land,
all glowing and white
as a candle burning so bright
there to tell you:

"Fear not, you have not to walk alone in this world.
There is someone who will love forever and care for

always; one to light a fire during the storm, to be a shoulder to cry on, a ground to walk upon. He died to give you life. He truly saved yours and mine. Follow Him and He will make your path straight."

You ask, "Who is this someone you speak so highly of?"

Then a strong, yet gentle voice arises from the man in white in front of you:

"I am Jesus Christ. I am the Son of God, the Savior of men, here to save you from your sins and give you eternal life."

Then you ask, "How do I get hold of this 'eternal life?'"

"You pray. You say something like:

'Father, I know I have sinned, but I also know you can forgive them. I want this eternal life. I want to live in Heaven in the mansion you will prepare for me. Lord, I know I cannot live this life alone. I ask you into my heart and that's where you will stay. I love you. God, my Savior and Friend.'"

"So, that's all I need to do?" you say, looking for more.

"Yes, it's that simple," the gentle, kind man says.

You kneel to pray. "Your life is saved.

Now you can live eternally."

Make a choice.

It's up to you, to live in Heaven or to burn a painful death in hell.

The choice is yours and yours alone.

I have eternal life. Do you?

APPENDIX C

Prayer of Salvation

If it is your desire to secure your eternal destiny in Heaven by professing your faith in the Lord Jesus Christ (Yeshua), below is a suggested prayer you can pray. There is no magic in these words, however God will hear the sincerity of your heart.

Heavenly Father, I thank You for loving me so much that You sent Your Son Jesus as the Way for me to receive forgiveness of sins and be released from the power of sin, Satan and death.

I confess that I am a sinner. I believe that Jesus died for my sins and was raised from the dead. I no longer wish to go my own way.

I renounce the works of the devil in my life. I repent and receive Jesus's perfection in exchange for my sins.

I ask Jesus to come into my heart to be my Savior and Lord. I humbly ask that You fill me with Your Holy Spirit and give me power from on high to follow You all the days of my life.

In Jesus's name I pray. Amen.

If you just prayed this prayer, welcome to the eternal Family of God and the Body of Christ—His Bride-Church! Luke 15:10 says that the angels in Heaven rejoice over one sinner who repents!

Your new brothers and sisters in Christ desire to rejoice with you as well. Tell them about your decision! Find a Bible teaching church community and Bible Study group who will love you and help you grow in your newfound relationship with our Lord and Savior Jesus Christ.

NOTES

SPLENDID; ADJECTIVE

1. www.merriam-webster.com

1. A MATCH MADE IN HEAVEN

1. Author's Parenthesis
2. See John 2:1-11
3. See Revelation 22:17
4. Nicholl, Colin R., *The Great Christ Comet: Revealing the True Star of Bethlehem* (Wheaton: Crossway; 1st edition, 2015).
5. See Psalm 102:25
6. See Jeremiah 31:3
7. See Mark 1:10-11
8. See Genesis 1:26-31
9. See Genesis 2:7
10. Note: Jewels symbolize rewards each will receive at the Judgment of believers' works. See 1 Corinthians 3:12-14
11. See Matthew 22:30; Psalm 16:11
12. Strong, James, *The New Strong's Expanded Exhaustive Concordance of the Bible* (Nashville, Thomas Nelson; Expanded edition, 2010), H3068.
13. See Mark 12:37a
14. Strong, James, *The New Strong's Expanded Exhaustive Concordance of the Bible* (Nashville, Thomas Nelson; Expanded edition, 2010), G2962.
15. See 1 Peter 3:6
16. See 1 Corinthians 11:25
17. See Matthew 1:20. Joseph considered quietly divorcing Mary upon learning that she had conceived a child, however, God intervened.
18. Kasdan, Barney, *God's Appointed Customs: A Messianic Jewish Guide to the Biblical Lifecycle and Lifestyle* (Baltimore: Messianic Jewish Publishers, 1996), 47-63.

2. FRACTURED FAIRY TALE

1. Strong, James, *The New Strong's Expanded Exhaustive Concordance of the Bible* (Nashville, Thomas Nelson; Expanded edition, 2010), H5730.
2. Rheims, Douay, *The Douay-Rheims Bible, 1899 American Edition* (Edinburgh: CrossReach Publications, 2016).
3. See Genesis 2:9-12
4. See Genesis 2:16
5. See 1 Corinthians 15:50
6. See Genesis 24:1-53
7. See Genesis 29:14-30
8. See Luke 22:47-48
9. See Numbers 30:10-16
10. Strong, James, *The New Strong's Expanded Exhaustive Concordance of the Bible* (Nashville, Thomas Nelson; Expanded edition, 2010), H3722.
11. See Hebrews 4:15
12. See 1 Corinthians 7:12-17
13. See 1 Corinthians 12:27
14. Strong, James, *The New Strong's Expanded Exhaustive Concordance of the Bible* (Nashville, Thomas Nelson; Expanded edition, 2010), H6763.
15. See 1 Corinthians 6:17; Amos 3:3; Romans 5:5b
16. Strong, James, *The New Strong's Expanded Exhaustive Concordance of the Bible* (Nashville, Thomas Nelson; Expanded edition, 2010), G4125.
17. See Malachi 2:16
18. Hawthorne, Nathaniel, *The Scarlet Letter* (New York: Holt, Rinehart and Winston, 1947), 56.
19. See Deuteronomy 5:6-22
20. See Matthew 27:26-31
21. See 2 Corinthians 5:21
22. See Revelation 7:9, 14

3. GOD'S DIVINE SOLUTION

1. See Matthew 3:17, 17:5; Mark 1:11, 9:7; Luke 3:22; 2 Peter 1:17
2. Strong, James, *The New Strong's Expanded Exhaustive Concordance of the Bible* (Nashville, Thomas Nelson; Expanded edition, 2010), G27.
3. See 2 Corinthians 5:16
4. See Ephesians 1:13-14
5. See Luke 4:1
6. See Exodus 40:34, 2 Chronicles 7:1
7. See Romans 3:25
8. See Leviticus 16:2c
9. See Galatians 4:6a
10. See Romans 2:15

11. See Matthew 27:50-51
12. Strong, James, *The New Strong's Expanded Exhaustive Concordance of the Bible* (Nashville, Thomas Nelson; Expanded edition, 2010), H5315.
13. See Nehemiah 2:17
14. See John 2:14-16, Matthew 21:13
15. See Genesis 22:11-14a
16. See Galatians 3:6
17. Chapman, Gary, *The Five Love Languages* (Chicago: Northfield Publishing, 2020).
18. Strong, James, *The New Strong's Expanded Exhaustive Concordance of the Bible* (Nashville, Thomas Nelson; Expanded edition, 2010), G2962.

4. LOOK IN THE MIRROR

1. See Hebrews 7:27
2. See 1 Corinthians 15:33
3. Bill McCartney is the founder of the Promise Keepers men's ministry. He is also former head football coach at the University of Colorado Boulder.
4. See Luke 2:21-24
5. See Colossians 2:12
6. See Luke 23:39-43
7. Graham, Billy, *The Holy Spirit: Activating God's Power in Your Life* (Waco: Word, 1975), 110-113.
8. See 2 Samuel 11
9. See Galatians 5:20; Ephesians 4:31; Colossians 3:8; Romans 1:29; 1 Peter 2:1; Titus 3:3
10. www.dictionary.com
11. Unger, Merrill F., *The New Unger's Bible Dictionary* (Chicago: Moody Publishers, 2006).
12. See Leviticus 26:40-42
13. See Romans 2:15
14. See Matthew 26:69-75
15. See John 21:15-25
16. See Jeremiah 8:12
17. See Genesis 29:16-25
18. See Genesis 29:17
19. See John 8:44
20. See Hebrews 12:2
21. See Ephesians 3:6
22. See Revelation 7:17; 21:6; 22:1
23. See John 4:6-42

5. TAKE A CLOSER LOOK

1. See Matthew 7:3-5
2. See Matthew 5:27-28
3. See Luke 23:34a
4. Tibbitts, Dana, and Goldberg, Patti, *Off the Hook: How Forgiving You Frees Me* (Somis: Whitestone Publishing, 2019).
5. *Stanley, Charles F., The Gift of Forgiveness* (Nashville: Thomas Nelson, 2002).

6. ACHIEVING AN INNER RADIANCE

1. See Ephesians 5:18
2. See Hebrews 9:4
3. See Exodus 16:1-36
4. See Deuteronomy 27-28
5. See Hebrews 4:12
6. See Numbers 17:8, 10
7. See John 14:23
8. Casper, Jayson. "The Top 50 Countries Where It's Hardest to Be a Christian (2020)." Posted January 15, 2020. *Christianity Today Online.* https://www.christianitytoday.com/news/2020/january/top-christian-persecution-open-doors-2020-world-watch-list.html
9. See James 1:2-4
10. See Luke 22:31
11. See Job 1:6-12

7. OBTAINING AN OUTER GLOW

1. See Exodus 34:14
2. Strong, James, *The New Strong's Expanded Exhaustive Concordance of the Bible* (Nashville, Thomas Nelson; Expanded edition, 2010), H7065.
3. See Genesis 31:32
4. See Exodus 32
5. See Joshua 1:7
6. See Ephesians 5:23
7. Strong, James, *The New Strong's Expanded Exhaustive Concordance of the Bible* (Nashville, Thomas Nelson; Expanded edition, 2010), G3404.

8. BECOMING A BRILLIANT REFLECTION

1. Strong, James, *The New Strong's Expanded Exhaustive Concordance of the Bible* (Nashville, Thomas Nelson; Expanded edition, 2010), G3933.
2. See Psalm 119:105
3. See 1 Samuel 16:13
4. See Acts 8:18-22
5. See 2 Corinthians 1:21-22; Hebrews 13:5
6. Strong, James, *The New Strong's Expanded Exhaustive Concordance of the Bible* (Nashville, Thomas Nelson; Expanded edition, 2010), 3474.
7. Strong, James, *The New Strong's Expanded Exhaustive Concordance of the Bible* (Nashville, Thomas Nelson; Expanded edition, 2010), 1127.
8. See Romans 1:20
9. See Romans 2:15
10. See Romans 3:23
11. See James 3:17
12. See John 3:34
13. See Ephesians 5:15-20
14. See Ephesians 5:18-20
15. See 1 John 2:15-17
16. See Luke 23:43
17. See 1 Corinthians 15:22-24a
18. Strong, James, *The New Strong's Expanded Exhaustive Concordance of the Bible* (Nashville, Thomas Nelson; Expanded edition, 2010), G536.
19. See Zephaniah 3:12-13
20. See Micah 2:12-13
21. See Revelation 7:1-8
22. Walvoord, John F., & Zuck, Roy B., *The Bible Knowledge Commentary: An Exposition of the Scriptures by Dallas Seminary Faculty* [New Testament Edition] (Colorado Springs: Chariot Victor Publishing, 1983), 964.
23. See Revelation 14:1-5
24. See Revelation 3:16
25. See John 15:13-15
26. See 1 Corinthians 6:15-20
27. See 1 Corinthians 7:3-5
28. See Numbers 14:34
29. See Romans 12:1-2
30. See Philippians 3:8
31. See Deuteronomy 29:4, Acts 28:27
32. See Hebrews 4:12
33. See John 21:17
34. See John 4:23-24
35. Strong, James, *The New Strong's Expanded Exhaustive Concordance of the Bible* (Nashville, Thomas Nelson; Expanded edition, 2010), G2999.
36. See Colossians 3:23

37. See James 5:16
38. See Hebrews 4:1,3, 9-11
39. See Exodus 33:7-11

9. THE ROYAL WEDDING IN HEAVEN

1. See Genesis 17
2. See Genesis 14:17-20; Hebrews 7
3. Vos, Howard F., *New Illustrated Bible Manners & Customs* (Nashville: Thomas Nelson, 1991), 17
4. See Genesis 15:6
5. See Jeremiah 34:18-19
6. See Genesis 15
7. Walvoord, John F. & Zuck, Roy B., *The Bible Knowledge Commentary: Old Testament Edition* (Colorado Springs: Chariot Victor Publishing, 1985) 58
8. See Ephesians 2:8-9
9. See Hebrews 9:15
10. See Romans 2:29
11. See Luke 1:31-33; Revelation 19:6; Isaiah 9:6; Matthew 9:6; Mark 15:26
12. Strong, James, *The New Strong's Expanded Exhaustive Concordance of the Bible* (Nashville, Thomas Nelson; Expanded edition, 2010), G726.
13. Miller Jr., Brent, director. 2020. *Before the Wrath.* Ingenuity Films.
14. Gregg, Steve, *Revelation: Four Views, Revised and Updated eBook* (Nashville: Thomas Nelson, 2020).
15. Rosenthal, Marvin, *The Pre-Wrath Rapture of the Church* (Nashville: Thomas Nelson, 1990).
16. See Revelation 20:4-6
17. For further study on the Timing of the Rapture see: Amos 7:1; Daniel 7:25, 11:35, 12:10; Zechariah 12:10-13:1; Matthew 24:30-31; 1 Corinthians 15:22-24; 1 Thessalonians 4:15-17; 2 Thessalonians 2:1-5; and Revelation 9:3-4, 13:7-10
18. See Revelation 6:10-11
19. See Revelation 7:9-14
20. See Revelation 19:7b-8
21. See Revelation 15:6; Leviticus 6:10
22. Strong, James, *The New Strong's Expanded Exhaustive Concordance of the Bible* (Nashville, Thomas Nelson; Expanded edition, 2010), G2513.
23. See Numbers 31:23, 1 Corinthians 3:12-15
24. Strong's G3408
25. See John 3:29; Revelation 18:20, 19:4
26. See Psalm 89:14, Job 29:14

10. THE HEAVENLY WEDDING FEAST

1. See Daniel 9:25-26
2. Author's Parenthesis
3. See Luke 13:30
4. Strong, James, *The New Strong's Expanded Exhaustive Concordance of the Bible* (Nashville, Thomas Nelson; Expanded edition, 2010), G3567.
5. See Matthew 9:15; Mark 2:19; Luke 5:34
6. See Ruth 3
7. See Genesis 29:27
8. See Ephesians 5:30
9. See Matthew 22:30
10. Strong, James, *The New Strong's Expanded Exhaustive Concordance of the Bible* (Nashville, Thomas Nelson; Expanded edition, 2010), G1097.
11. Strong, James, *The New Strong's Expanded Exhaustive Concordance of the Bible* (Nashville, Thomas Nelson; Expanded edition, 2010), G1921.
12. See 1 Peter 1:8
13. See Psalm 16:11
14. See Genesis 18
15. See Psalm 78:24-25
16. See Luke 24:42

11. THE REIGN OF JESUS ON THE EARTH

1. See Revelation 11:1-12
2. See John 1:21
3. See Revelation 11:7-12
4. See Revelation 13:11-18
5. See Isaiah 63:1-3a
6. See 2 Thessalonians 2:13; Revelation 14:1-4
7. See Romans 11:25-30
8. See Zechariah 14:16-19
9. Walvoord, John F., & Zuck, Roy B., *The Bible Knowledge Commentary: Old Testament Edition* (Colorado Springs: Chariot Victor Publishing, 1985), 293.
10. See Matthew 13:29-30; Judges 15:1
11. See Joel 3:13
12. For further study on the Wheat and Grape Harvests you can look at Matthew 3:12, 13:24-30, 13:36-43; Isaiah 63:1-3; Joel 3:12-13; Revelation 14:14-20, 19:15-21
13. Strong, James, *The New Strong's Expanded Exhaustive Concordance of the Bible* (Nashville, Thomas Nelson; Expanded edition, 2010), G444.
14. Strong, James, *The New Strong's Expanded Exhaustive Concordance of the Bible* (Nashville, Thomas Nelson; Expanded edition, 2010), G3567.

15. Strong, James, *The New Strong's Expanded Exhaustive Concordance of the Bible* (Nashville, Thomas Nelson; Expanded edition, 2010), G3624.
16. See Mark 11:17
17. See Daniel 12:13
18. See Daniel 12:11-12; Revelation 13:5,7,9b
19. See Revelation 20:4-6
20. See Joshua 2
21. See Revelation 6-19
22. See Daniel 7:27; 1 Corinthians 6:2-3; Revelation 2:26
23. See Revelation 19:12a
24. See Revelation 4:10-11
25. See 2 Peter 3:11-13
26. See 1 Corinthians 2:9
27. See 1 Peter 2:5; Ephesians 2:20-22, also Zechariah 8:9

12. ARISE AND SHINE

1. Evans, Jimmy, *Tipping Point—The End is Here* (Dallas: XO Publishing, 2020), 41.
2. See Matthew 5:16, Author's Paraphrase
3. See Revelation 22:16
4. See Matthew 14:13-21
5. See Romans 12:6-8; 11:29
6. See Ephesians 4:1-12
7. See 1 Corinthians 12:1-30
8. Hayford, Jack, *Explaining the Trinity* (Lancaster, United Kingdom: Sovereign World Ltd, 2003), 37.
9. See Romans 10:17
10. See 2 Timothy 3:16, 2 Peter 1:21
11. See Exodus 3:14
12. "Eternal Life" by Hannah Davis can be found in Appendix B of this book.
13. See 1 Corinthians 1:19
14. Dostoyevsky, Fyodor, Constance Garnett, and Ernest J. Simmons, *Crime and Punishment* (New York: Modern Library, 1950).
15. See Revelation 3:11, 22:7, 22:12, 22:20
16. Strong, James, *The New Strong's Expanded Exhaustive Concordance of the Bible* (Nashville, Thomas Nelson; Expanded edition, 2010), G5035.

ABOUT THE AUTHORS

Mary Soler is an author, speaker, and Bible teacher with more than 26 years of experience presenting in-depth, large-group Bible curriculum for Community Bible Study (CBS). Mary has served in a variety of roles for CBS, including Los Angeles Area Director, Teaching Director and Founding Director. Mary is known for her accurate Bible exposition and keen eschatological understanding of biblical concepts, prophecy, and history.

Joseph served 16 years in leadership with Community Bible Study as an Associate Teaching Director and Senior Leader.

From 2006 to 2008, Mary and her husband Joseph, hosted a weekly radio broadcast called *Return of the King*. This teaching series walked radio listeners through prophetic, End-Times Scriptures, delving into the depths of Revelation and Daniel.

Both Mary and Joseph are passionate about discipling followers of Christ. They delight in seeing believers grow in their love and knowledge of the Lord Jesus Christ.

Mary and Joseph have been married for more than 41 years and are blessed with three children and five grandchildren. Originally from Southern California, they now reside in a suburb of San Antonio, Texas.

Connect with Mary Soler at www.marysoler.com

Made in the USA
Columbia, SC
22 October 2021